Learning Neo4j

Run blazingly fast queries on complex graph datasets
with the power of the Neo4j graph database

Rik Van Bruggen

[PACKT] open source*
community experience distilled

PUBLISHING

BIRMINGHAM - MUMBAI

Learning Neo4j

First published: August 2014

Production reference: 1190814

Published by Packt Publishing Ltd.
Livery Place
35 Livery Street
Birmingham B3 2PB, UK.

ISBN 978-1-84951-716-4

www.packtpub.com

Cover image by Pratyush Mohanta (tysoncinematics@gmail.com)

Credits

Author
Rik Van Bruggen

Reviewers
Jussi Heinonen

Michael Hunger

Andreas Kolleger

Max De Marzi

Mark Needham

Yavor Stoychev

Ron Van Weverwijk

Acquisition Editor
Nikhil Karkal

Content Development Editor
Poonam Jain

Technical Editors
Tanvi Bhatt

Akash Rajiv Sharma

Faisal Siddiqui

Aman Preet Singh

Copy Editors
Roshni Banerjee

Sayanee Mukherjee

Aditya Nair

Deepa Nambiar

Project Coordinator
Mary Alex

Proofreaders
Simran Bhogal

Maria Gould

Ameesha Green

Paul Hindle

Indexers
Hemangini Bari

Tejal Soni

Priya Subramani

Graphics
Sheetal Aute

Ronak Dhruv

Valentina D'silva

Disha Haria

Abhinash Sahu

Production Coordinator
Komal Ramchandani

Cover Work
Komal Ramchandani

About the Author

Rik Van Bruggen is the regional territory manager for Neo Technology for Benelux, UK, and the Nordic region. He has been working for startup companies for most of his career, including eCom Interactive Expertise, SilverStream Software, Imprivata, and Courion. While he has an interest in technology, his real passion is business and how to make technology work for a business. He lives in Antwerp, Belgium, with his wife and three lovely kids, and enjoys technology, orienteering, jogging, and Belgian beer.

This book and all of the work that went on around it would not have been possible without the unconditional support of my wife, Katleen, and our three lovely kids, Mit, Toon, and Cas. Thank you!

About the Reviewers

Michael Hunger has been passionate about software development for a long time. He is particularly interested in the people who develop software, software craftsmanship, programming languages, and improving code.

For the past few years, he has been working with Neo Technology on the Neo4j graph database. As the project lead of Spring Data Neo4j, he helped develop the idea to make it a convenient and complete solution for object graph mapping. He now takes care of all the aspects of the Neo4j developer community.

Good relationships are everywhere in Michael's life. His life revolves around his family and children, running his coffee shop and co-working space, having fun in the depths of a text-based, multiuser dungeon, tinkering with and without Lego, and much more.

As a developer, he loves to work with many aspects of programming languages—learning new things every day, participating in exciting and ambitious open source projects, and contributing and writing software-related books and articles. He is also an active speaker at conferences and events, and a longtime editor at InfoQ.

He is one of the important contributors to the expert book, *97 Things Every Programmer Should Know* by *Kevin Henney, O'Reilly*.

He has co-authored *Spring Data*, by *Mark Pollack, Oliver Gierke, Thomas Risberg,* and *Jon Brisbin, O'Reilly* and has also reviewed the following books:

- *NoSQL Distilled, Pramod J. Sadalage and Martin Fowler, Pearson*
- *Domain-Specific Languages Patterns, Martin Fowler and Rebecca Parsons, Pearson*
- *Pragmatic Guide to Git, Travis Swicegood, The Pragmatic Bookshelf*
- *Art of Readable Code, Dustin Boswell and Trevor Foucher, O'Reilly*
- *Apprenticeship Patterns, David H. Hoover and Adewale Oshineye, O'Reilly*

> I want to thank the four wonderful women in my life who make me happy every day and let me achieve many things.

Ron Van Weverwijk is an experienced software developer at GoDataDriven in Netherlands. He has years of experience developing both backend and frontend applications.

For the last few years, he has been building applications to explore and visualize complex network data using Neo4j. He is an expert Neo4j developer and community member. He has given several Neo4j trainings, and has spoken about Neo4j at a number of recent conferences.

www.PacktPub.com

Support files, eBooks, discount offers and more

You might want to visit www.PacktPub.com for support files and downloads related to your book.

Did you know that Packt offers eBook versions of every book published, with PDF and ePub files available? You can upgrade to the eBook version at www.PacktPub.com and as a print book customer, you are entitled to a discount on the eBook copy. Get in touch with us at service@packtpub.com for more details.

At www.PacktPub.com, you can also read a collection of free technical articles, sign up for a range of free newsletters and receive exclusive discounts and offers on Packt books and eBooks.

http://PacktLib.PacktPub.com

Do you need instant solutions to your IT questions? PacktLib is Packt's online digital book library. Here, you can access, read and search across Packt's entire library of books.

Why Subscribe?
- Fully searchable across every book published by Packt
- Copy and paste, print and bookmark content
- On demand and accessible via web browser

Free Access for Packt account holders

If you have an account with Packt at www.PacktPub.com, you can use this to access PacktLib today and view nine entirely free books. Simply use your login credentials for immediate access.

"To Katleen, Mit, Toon, and Cas"

–with love, Rik

Table of Contents

Preface

The title of this book, *Learning Neo4j*, is a really good title in many ways. On one hand, it reflects my own personal experience with Neo4j over the past couple of years and more. As I fell deeply in love with graph technology, Neo4j kept on providing me with new fascinating things to learn about and explore. This book, in more than one way, is a summary of that learning experience—it's the tale of my *learning* of Neo4j.

But the book is also supposed to provide you with lots of good starting points to get going with this technology more quickly. I know for a fact that finding learning resources on these types of technologies is not always easy, and that's really what drove me personally to spend many late nights, weekends, and holidays to put together this book to accelerate *your* learning of Neo4j.

What this book covers

Chapter 1, Graphs and Graph Theory – an Introduction, provides you with some background information on graphs to help you understand where the technology behind Neo4j came from.

Chapter 2, Graph Databases – Overview, will try to explain how the theory of the previous chapter is used to create a new, different kind of database that is "standing on the shoulders of giants". We are going to be basing ourselves on several decades of database technologies, of course.

Chapter 3, Getting Started with Neo4j, gives you an overview of several of Neo4j's key characteristics, and then helps you get going with the tool on different on-premise and cloud-based platforms.

Chapter 4, Modeling Data for Neo4j, will provide you with an introduction to data modeling for graph databases. Before you take your newly acquired tool (discussed in the previous chapter) for a spin, you need to think about the data model, just as you would with any other database.

Chapter 5, Importing Data into Neo4j, will give you a good look at the different options and considerations to import data into your newly created model (discussed in *Chapter 4, Modeling Data for Neo4j*). It will show you some of the different import techniques in detail as well.

Chapters 6, Use Case Example – Recommendations, will provide detailed examples of use cases for Neo4j that seem to have become quite commonplace in many different industries. This chapter focuses on recommendations.

Chapter 7, Use Case Example – Impact Analysis and Simulation, will take a deep look into the impact analysis use cases of Neo4j.

Chapter 8, Visualizations for Neo4j, will give you an overview of how to integrate the Neo4j graph database with the powerful domain of graph visualizations. We will discuss different alternatives, and point you to different resources to get started with.

Chapter 9, Other Tools Related to Neo4j, will provide you with some pointers to interesting complementary tools that relate to Neo4j, such as data integration tools, business intelligence tools, and modeling tools.

Appendix A, Where to Find More Information Related to Neo4j, gives a basic introduction to Cypher.

Appendix B, Getting Started with Cypher, discusses the Neo4j query language that we are using throughout the book.

What you need for this book

This book can be read without any additional resources; however, we recommend access to some physical lab resources to install Neo4j Community Edition on. You can download that software from `http://neo4j.com/download/` at your convenience.

A reasonable and recommended lab setup can be one on a machine with a dual or quad-core processor with 8 GB of RAM. A system with a lesser configuration would probably also work, but the recommended one will make it more comfortable for you.

Also note that you need OpenJDK 7 (`http://openjdk.java.net/`) or Oracle Java 7 (`http://www.oracle.com/technetwork/java/javase/downloads/index.html`) installed on your machine.

Who this book is for

If you are an IT professional or developer who wants to get started in the field of graph databases, this is the book for you. Anyone with prior experience with SQL in the relational database world will very quickly feel at ease with Neo4j and its Cypher query language and learn a lot from this book.

Conventions

In this book, you will find a number of styles of text that distinguish between different kinds of information. Here are some examples of these styles, and an explanation of their meaning.

Code words in text, database table names, folder names, filenames, file extensions, pathnames, dummy URLs, user input, and Twitter handles are shown as follows: "As explained previously, the output of the batch importer is not what we will immediately see on our Neo4j server. In fact, the output is just a `test.db` directory."

A block of code is set as follows:

```
//Loading CSV with Rels
load csv with headers from
"file:/your/path/to/rels.csv"
as rels
match (from {id: rels.From}), (to {id: rels.To})
create from-[:REL {type: rels.`Relationship Type`}]->to
return from, to
```

Any command-line input or output is written as follows:

```
cd /path/to/your/Neo4j/server
curl http://dist.Neo4j.org/jexp/shell/Neo4j-shell-tools-2.0.zip -o Neo4j-shell-tools.zip
unzip Neo4j-shell-tools.zip -d lib
```

New terms and **important words** are shown in bold. Words that you see on the screen, in menus or dialog boxes for example, appear in the text like this: "The **Admin** panel shows us the way, and gives immediate access to this particular Neo4j instance's browser interface."

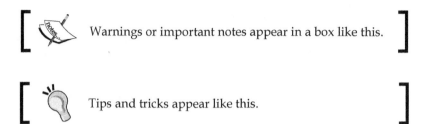

Warnings or important notes appear in a box like this.

Tips and tricks appear like this.

Reader feedback

Feedback from our readers is always welcome. Let us know what you think about this book—what you liked or may have disliked. Reader feedback is important for us to develop titles that you really get the most out of.

To send us general feedback, simply send an e-mail to feedback@packtpub.com, and mention the book title via the subject of your message.

If there is a topic that you have expertise in and you are interested in either writing or contributing to a book, see our author guide on www.packtpub.com/authors.

Customer support

Now that you are the proud owner of a Packt book, we have a number of things to help you to get the most from your purchase.

Downloading the color images of this book

We also provide you a PDF file that has color images of the screenshots/diagrams used in this book. The color images will help you better understand the changes in the output. You can download this file from https://www.packtpub.com/sites/default/files/downloads/7164OS_GraphicsBundle.pdf.

Errata

Although we have taken every care to ensure the accuracy of our content, mistakes do happen. If you find a mistake in one of our books—maybe a mistake in the text or the code—we would be grateful if you would report this to us. By doing so, you can save other readers from frustration and help us improve subsequent versions of this book. If you find any errata, please report them by visiting http://www.packtpub.com/submit-errata, selecting your book, clicking on the **errata submission form** link, and entering the details of your errata. Once your errata are verified, your submission will be accepted and the errata will be uploaded on our website, or added to any list of existing errata, under the Errata section of that title. Any existing errata can be viewed by selecting your title from http://www.packtpub.com/support.

Piracy

Piracy of copyright material on the Internet is an ongoing problem across all media. At Packt, we take the protection of our copyright and licenses very seriously. If you come across any illegal copies of our works, in any form, on the Internet, please provide us with the location address or website name immediately so that we can pursue a remedy.

Please contact us at copyright@packtpub.com with a link to the suspected pirated material.

We appreciate your help in protecting our authors, and our ability to bring you valuable content.

Questions

You can contact us at questions@packtpub.com if you are having a problem with any aspect of the book, and we will do our best to address it.

1
Graphs and Graph Theory – an Introduction

People have different ways of learning new topics. We know that background information can contribute greatly to a better understanding of new topics. That is why, in this chapter of our *Learning Neo4j* book, we will start with quite a bit of background information, not to recount the tales of history, but to give you the necessary context that can lead to a better understanding of topics.

In order to do so, we will address the following topics:

- **Graphs**: What they are and where they came from. This section will aim to set the record straight on what exactly our subject will contain and what it won't.

- **Graph theory**: What it is and what it is used for. This section will give you quite a few examples of graph theory applications, and it will also start hinting at applications for graph databases such as Neo4j later on.

So, let's dig right in.

Introduction to and history of graphs

Many people might have used the word *graph* at some point in their professional or personal lives. However, chances are that they did not use it in the way that we will be using it in this book. Most people—obviously not you, my dear reader, otherwise you probably would not have picked up this book—actually think about something very different when talking about a graph. They think about pie charts and bar charts. They think about graphics, not graphs.

In this book, we will be working with a completely different type of subject—the graphs that you might know from your math classes. I, for once, distinctly remember being taught the basics of discrete Mathematics in one of my university classes, and I also remember finding it terribly complex and difficult to work with. Little did I know that my later professional career will use these techniques in a software context, let alone that I would be writing a book on this topic.

So, what are graphs? To explain this, I think it is useful to put a little historic context around the concept. Graphs are actually quite old as a concept. They were invented, or at least first described, in an academic paper by the well-known Swiss mathematician Leonhard Euler. He was trying to solve an age-old problem that we now know as the *7 bridges of Königsberg*. The problem at hand was pretty simple to understand.

Königsberg has a beautiful medieval city in the Prussian empire, situated on the river Pregel. It is located between Poland and Lithuania in today's Russia. If you try to look it up on any modern-day map, you will most likely not find it as it is currently known as Kaliningrad. The Pregel not only cut Königsberg into a left- and right-bank side of the city, but it also created an island in the middle of the river, which was known as the Kneiphof. The result of this peculiar situation was a city that was cut into four parts. We will refer to them as A, B, C and D, which were connected by seven bridges (labeled a, b, c, d, e, f, and g in the following diagram).This gives us the following situation:

- The seven bridges are connected to the four different parts of the city
- The essence of the problem that people were trying to solve was to take a tour of the city, visiting every one of its parts and crossing every single one of its bridges, without having to walk a single bridge or street twice

In the following diagram, you can see how Euler illustrated this problem in his original 1736 paper:

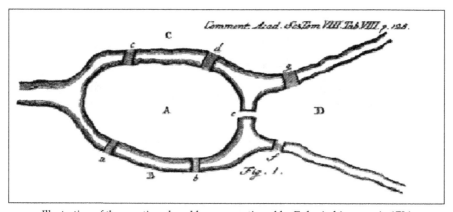

Illustration of the mentioned problem as mentioned by Euler in his paper in 1736

Essentially, it was a pathfinding problem, like there are many others (for example, the **knight's ride** problem or the **travelling salesman** problem). It does not seem like a very difficult assignment at all now does it? However, at the time, people really struggled with it and were trying to figure it out for the longest time. It was not until Euler got involved and took a very different, mathematical approach to the problem that it got solved once and for all.

Euler did the following two things that I find really interesting:

1. First and foremost, he decided not to take the traditional brute force method to solve the problem (that is, in this case, drawing a number of different route options on the map and trying to figure out—essentially by trial and error—if there was such a route through the city), but decided to do something different. He took a step back and took a different look at the problem by creating what I call an *abstract version* of the problem at hand, which is essentially a model of the problem domain that he was trying to work with. In his mind at least, Euler must have realized that the citizens of Königsberg were focusing their attention on the wrong part of the problem—the streets. Euler quickly came to the conclusion that the streets of Königsberg really did not matter to find a solution to the problem. The only things that mattered for his pathfinding operation were the following:

    ◦   The parts of the city
    ◦   The bridges connecting the parts of the city

    Now, all of a sudden, we seem to have a very different problem at hand, which can be accurately represented in what is often regarded as "the world's first graph":

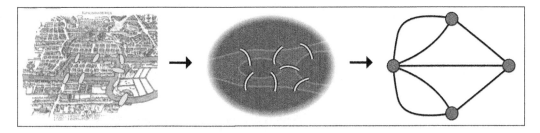

2. Secondly, Euler solved the puzzle at hand by applying a mathematical algorithm on the model that he created. Euler's logic was simple: if I want to take a walk in the town of Königsberg, then:

    ◦   I will have to start somewhere in any one of the four parts of the city
    ◦   I will have to leave that part of the city; in other words, cross one of the bridges to go to another part of the city

 ° I will then have to cross another five bridges, leaving and entering different parts of the city

 ° Finally, I will end the walk through Königsberg in another part of the city

Therefore, Euler argues, the case must be that the first and last parts of the city have an odd number of bridges that connect them to other parts of the city (because you leave from the first part and you arrive at the last part of the city), but the other two parts of the city must have an even number of bridges connecting them to the first and last parts of the city because you will arrive *and* leave from these parts of the city.

This "number of bridges connecting the parts of the city" has a very special meaning in the model that Euler created, the graph representation of the model. We call this the degree of the nodes in the graph. In order for there to be a path through Königsberg that only crossed every bridge once, Euler proved that all he had to do was to apply a very simple algorithm that will establish the degree (in other words, count the number of bridges) of every part of the city. This is shown in the following diagram:

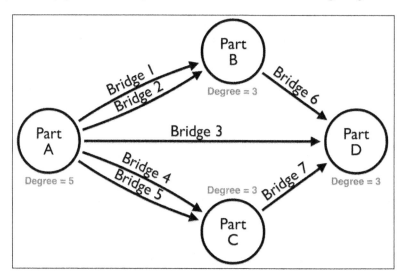

This is how Euler solved the famous "Seven bridges of Königsberg" problem. By proving that there was no part of the city that had an even number of bridges, he also proved that the required walk in the city cannot be done. Adding one more bridge would immediately make it possible, but with the current state of the city, and its bridges at the time, there was no way one could take such an **Eulerian Walk** of the city. By doing so, Euler created the world's first graph. The concepts and techniques of his research, however, are universally applicable; in order to do such a walk on any graph, the graph must have zero or two vertices with an odd degree, and all intermediate vertices must have an even degree.

To summarize, a graph is nothing more than an abstract, mathematical representation of two or more entities, which are somehow connected or related to each other. Graphs model pairwise relations between objects. They are, therefore, always made up of the following components:

- **The nodes of the graph, usually representing the objects mentioned previously**: In math, we usually refer to these structures as vertices; but for this book, and in the context of graph databases such as Neo4j, we will always refer to vertices as nodes.

- **The links between the nodes of the graph**: In math, we refer to these structures as edges, but again, for the purpose of this book, we will refer to these links as relationships.

- **The structure of how nodes and relationships are connected to each other makes a graph**: Many important qualities, such as the number of edges connected to a node, what we referred to as degree, can be assessed. Many other such indicators also exist.

Now that we have graphs and understand a bit more about their nature and history, it's time to look at the discipline that was created on top of these concepts, often referred to as the graph theory.

Definition and usage of graph theory

When Euler invented the first graph, he was trying to solve a very specific problem of the citizens of Königsberg, with a very specific representation/model and a very specific algorithm. It turns out that there are quite a few problems that can be:

- Described using the graph metaphor of objects and pairwise relations between these objects

- Solved by applying a mathematical algorithm to this structure

The mechanism is the same, and the scientific discipline that studies these modeling and solution patterns, using graphs, is often referred to as the graph theory, and it is considered to be a part of discrete Mathematics.

There are lots of different types of graphs that have been analyzed in this discipline, as you can see from the following diagram.

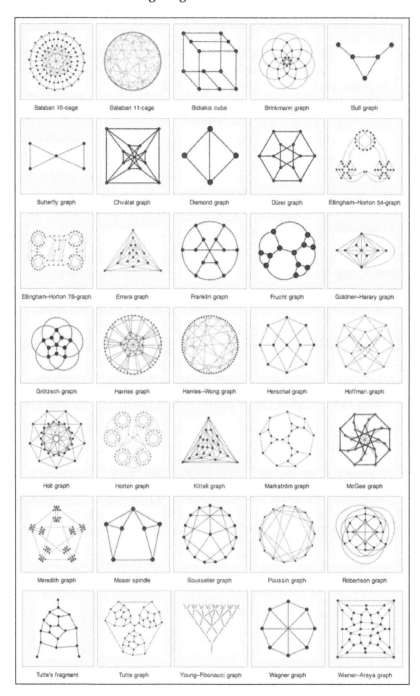

Graph theory, the study of graph models and algorithms, has turned out to be a fascinating field of study, which has been used in many different disciplines to solve some of the most interesting questions facing mankind. Interestingly enough, it has seldom really been applied with rigor in the different fields of science that can benefit from it; maybe scientists today don't have the multidisciplinary approach required (providing expertise from graph theory and their specific field of study) to do so.

So, let's talk about some of these fields of study a bit, without wanting to give you an exhaustive list of all applicable fields. Still, I do believe that some of these examples will be of interest for our future discussions in this book and work up an appetite for what types of applications we will use a graph-based database such as Neo4j for.

Social studies

For the longest time, people have understood that the way humans interact with one another is actually very easy to describe in a network. People interact with people every day. People influence one another every day. People exchange ideas every day. As they do, these interactions cause ripple effects through the social environment that they inhabit. Modeling these interactions as a graph has been of primary importance to better understand global demographics, political movements, and—last but not least—commercial adoption of certain products by certain groups. With the advent of online social networks, this graph-based approach to social understanding has taken a whole new direction. Companies such as Google, Facebook, Twitter, LinkedIn (see the following diagram featuring a visualization of my LinkedIn network), and many others have undertaken very specific efforts to include graph-based systems in the way they target their customers and users, and in doing so, they have changed many of our daily lives quite fundamentally.

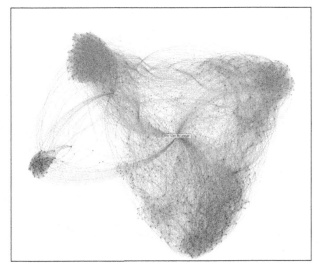

Biological studies

We sometimes say it in marketing taglines: "Graphs Are Everywhere". When we do so, we are actually describing reality in a very real and fascinating way. Also, in this field, researchers have known for quite some time that biological components (proteins, molecules, genes, and so on) and their interactions can accurately be modeled and described by means of a graph structure, and doing so yields many practical advantages. In metabolic pathways (see the following diagram for the human metabolic system), for example, graphs can help us to understand how the different parts of the human body interact with each other. In metaproteomics, researchers analyze how different kinds of proteins interact with one another and are used in order to better steer chemical and biological production processes.

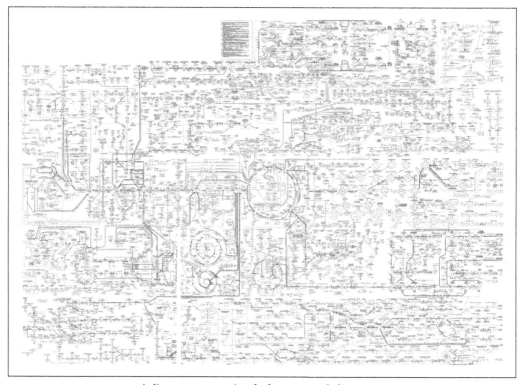

A diagram representing the human metabolic system

Computer science

Some of the earliest computers were built with graphs in mind. Graph Compute Engines solved scheduling problems for railroads as early as the late 19th century, and the usage of graphs in computer science has only accelerated since then. In today's applications, the use cases vary from chip design, network management, recommendation systems, and UML modeling to algorithm generation and dependency analysis. The following is an example of such a UML diagram:

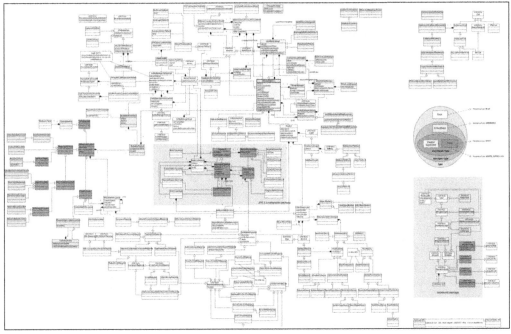

An example of a UML diagram

The latter is probably one of the more interesting use cases. Using pathfinding algorithms, software and hardware engineers have been analyzing the effects of changes in the design of their artifacts on the rest of the system. If a change is made to one part of the code, for example, a particular object is renamed; the dependency analysis algorithms can easily walk the graph of the system to find out what other classes will be affected by the former change.

Flow problems

Another really interesting field of graph theory applications is flow problems, also known as **maximum flow problems**. In essence, this field is part of a larger field of optimization problems, which is trying to establish the best possible path across a flow network. Flow networks are a type of graph in which the nodes/vertices of the graph are connected by relationships/edges that specify the capacity of that particular relationship. Examples can be found in fields such as telecom networks, gas networks, airline networks, package delivery networks, and many others, where graph-based models are then used in combination with complex algorithms. The following diagram is an example of such a network, as you can find it on `http://enipedia.tudelft.nl/`.

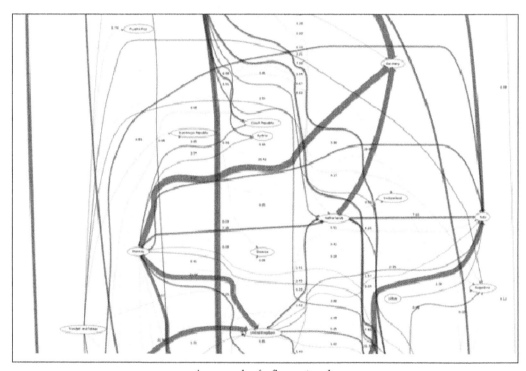

An example of a flow network

These algorithms are then used to identify the calculated optimal path, find bottlenecks, plan maintenance activities, conduct long-term capacity planning, and many other operations.

Route problems

The original problem that Euler set out to solve in 18th century Königsberg was in fact a route planning / pathfinding problem. Today, many graph applications leverage the extraordinary capability of graphs and graph algorithms to calculate — as opposed to finding with trial and error — the optimal route between two nodes on a network. In the following diagram, you will find a simple route planning example as a graph:

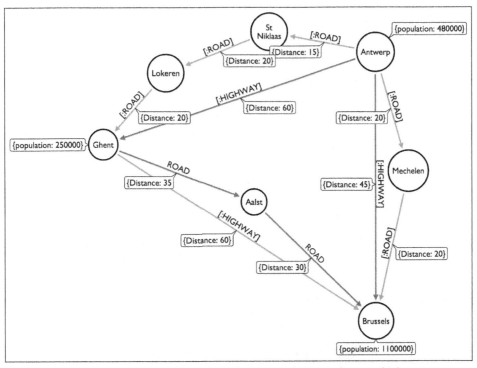

A simple route planning example between cities to choose roads versus highways

A very simple example will be from the domain of logistics. When trying to plan for the best way to get a package from one city to another, one will need the following:

1. A list of all routes available between the cities

2. The most optimal of the available routes, which depends on various parameters in the network, such as capacity, distance, cost, CO_2 exhaust, speed, and so on

This type of operation is a very nice use case for graph algorithms. There are a couple of very well-known algorithms that we can briefly highlight:

- **The Dijkstra algorithm**: This is one of the best-known algorithms to calculate the shortest weighted path between two points in a graph, using the properties of the edges as weights or costs of that link.

- **The A* (A-star) algorithm**: This is a variation of Dijkstra's original ideas, but it uses heuristics to predict more efficiently the shortest path explorations. As A* explores potential graph paths, it holds a sorted priority queue of alternate path segments along the way, since it calculates the "past path" cost and the "future path" cost of the different options that are possible during the route exploration.

Depending on the required result, the specific dataset, and the speed requirements, different algorithms will yield different returns.

Web search

No book chapter treating graphs and graph theory — even at the highest level — will be complete without mentioning one of the most powerful and widely-used graph algorithms on the planet, **PageRank**. PageRank is the original graph algorithm, invented by Google founder Larry Page in 1996 at Stanford University, to provide better web search results. For those of us old enough to remember the early days of web searching (using tools such as Lycos, AltaVista, and so on), it provided a true revolution in the way the Web was made accessible to end users. The following diagram represents the PageRank graph:

The older tools did keyword matching on web pages, but Google revolutionized this by no longer focusing on keywords alone, but by doing link analysis on the hyperlinks between different web pages. PageRank, and many of the other algorithms that Google uses today, assumes that more important web pages, which should appear higher in your search results, will have more incoming links from other pages, and therefore, it is able to score these pages by analyzing the graph of links to the web page. History has shown us the importance of PageRank. Not only has Google, Inc. built quite an empire on top of this graph algorithm, but its principles have also been applied to other fields such as cancer research and chemical reactions.

Test questions

Q1. Graph theory is a very recent field in modern Mathematics, invented in the late 20th century by Leonard Euler:

1. True
2. False

Q2. Name one field that graphs are NOT used for in today's science/application fields:

1. Route problems
2. Social studies
3. Accounting systems
4. Biological studies

Q3. Graphs are a very niche phenomenon that can only be applied to a very limited set of applications/research fields:

1. True
2. False

Summary

In the first chapter of this book, we wanted to give you a first look at some of the concepts that underpin the subject of this book, the graph database Neo4j. We introduced the history of graphs, explained some of the principles that are being explored in the fascinating mathematical field of graph theory, and provided some examples of other academic and functional domains that have been benefiting from this rich, century-long history. The conclusion of this is plain and simple: *Graphs Are Everywhere*. Much of our world is in reality dependent on and related to many other things — it is densely connected, as we call it in graph terms. This of course has implications on how we work with the reality in our computer systems, how we store the data that describes reality in a database management system, and how we interact with the system in different kinds of applications.

In the next chapter, we will start applying this context to the specific part of computer science that deals with graph structures in the field of database management systems.

Graph Databases – Overview

2

In this chapter, we want to contextualize the concepts around graph databases and make our readers understand the historical and operational differences between older, different kinds of database management systems and our modern-day Neo4j installations.

To do this, we will cover the following:

- Some background information on databases in general
- A walk-through of the different approaches taken to manage and store data, from old-school navigational databases to No-SQL graph databases
- A short discussion explaining the graph database category, its strengths, and its weaknesses

This chapter should then set our readers up for some more practical discussions later in this book.

Background

It's not always very clear when the first real database management system was formally conceived and implemented. Ever since Babbage invented the first complete Turing computing system (the Analytical Engine, which Babbage never really managed to get built), we have known that computers would always need to have some kind of memory. This will be responsible for dealing with the data upon which operations and calculations will be executed. But when did this memory evolve into a proper database? What do we mean by a database anyway?

Let's tackle the latter question first. A database can be described as any kind of organized collection of data. Not all databases require a management system—think of the many spreadsheets and other file-based storage approaches that really don't have any kind of real material oversight imposed on it, let alone a true management system. A database management system, then, can technically be referred to as a set of computer programs that manage (in the broadest sense of the word) the *database*. It is a system that sits between the user-facing hardware and software components and the data. It can be described as any system that is responsible for and able to manage the structure of the data, is able to store and retrieve that data, and provides access to this data in a correct, trustable, performant, secure fashion.

Databases as we know them, however, did not exist from the get-go of computing. At first, most computers used *memory*, and this memory used a special-purpose, custom-made storage format that often relied on very manual, labor-intensive, and hardware-based storage operations. Many systems relied on things like punch cards for its instructions and datasets. It's not that long ago that computer systems evolved from these seemingly ancient, special-purpose technologies.

Having read many different articles on this subject, I believe that the need for "general purpose" database management systems, similar to the ones that we know today, started to increase as:

- The number of computerized systems significantly increased
- A number of breakthroughs were realized in terms of computer memory. Direct Access memory—memory that would not have to rely on lots of winding of tapes or punched cards—became available in the middle of the 1960s.

Both of these elements were necessary preconditions for any kind of multipurpose database management system to make sense. The first real database management systems seem to have cropped up in the 1960s, and I believe it would be useful to quickly run through the different phases in the development of database management systems.

We can establish the following three major phases in the half century that database management systems have been under development:

- Navigational databases
- Relational databases
- NoSQL databases

Let's look at these three system types so that we can then more accurately position graph databases such as Neo4j—the real subject of this book.

Navigational databases

The original database management systems were developed by legendary computer scientists such as Charles Bachman, who gave a lot of thought to the way software should be built in a world of extremely scarce computing resources. Bachman invented a very natural (and as we will see later, graphical) way to model data: as a network of interrelated things. The starting point of such a database design was generally a *Bachman Diagram* (refer to the following diagram), which immediately feels like it expresses the model of the data structure in a very graph-like fashion:

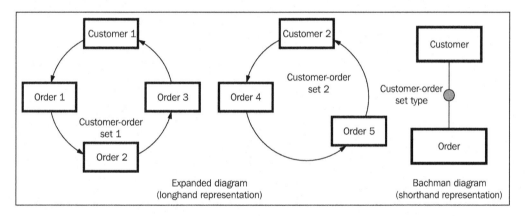

These diagrams were the starting points for database management systems that used either networks or hierarchies as the basic structure for their data. Both the network databases and the hierarchical database systems were built on the premise that data elements would be linked together by pointers.

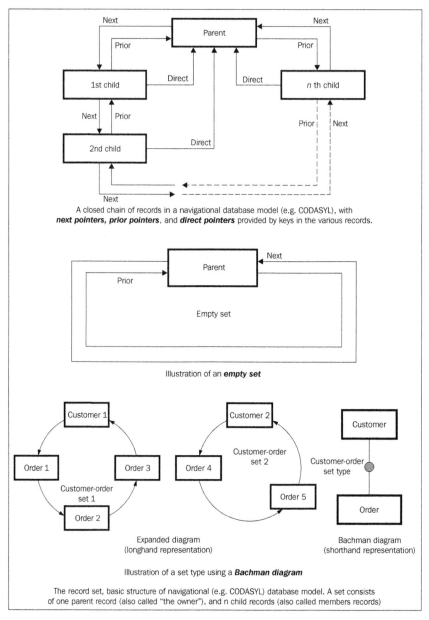

A closed chain of records in a navigational database model (e.g. CODASYL), with **next pointers, prior pointers**, and **direct pointers** provided by keys in the various records.

Illustration of an **empty set**

Expanded diagram
(longhand representation)

Bachman diagram
(shorthand representation)

Illustration of a set type using a **Bachman diagram**

The record set, basic structure of navigational (e.g. CODASYL) database model. A set consists of one parent record (also called "the owner"), and n child records (also called members records)

An example of a navigational database model with pointers linking records

As you can probably imagine from the preceding discussion, these models were very interesting and resulted in a number of efforts that shaped the database industry. One of these efforts was the Conference on Data Systems Languages, better known under its acronym, CODASYL. This played an ever so important role in the information technology industry of the sixties and seventies. It shaped one of the world's dominant computer programming systems (COBOL), but also provided the basis for a whole slew of navigational databases such as IDMS, Cullinet, and IMS. The latter, the IBM-backed IMS database, is often classified as a hierarchical database, which offers a subset of the network model of CODASYL.

Navigational databases eventually gave way to a new generation of databases, the Relational Database Management Systems. Many reasons have been attributed to this shift, some technical and some commercial, but the main two reasons that seem to enjoy agreement across the industry are:

- The complexity of the models that they used. CODASYL is widely regarded as something that can only be worked or understood by absolute experts—as we partly experienced in 1999, when the Y2K problem required many CODASYL experts to work overtime to migrate their systems into the new millennium.

- The lack of a declarative query mechanism for navigational database management systems. Most of those systems inherently provide a very imperative approach to finding data: the user would have to tell the database what to do instead of just being able to ask a question and having the database provide the answer.

This allows for a great transition from navigational to relational databases.

Relational databases

Relational Database Management Systems are probably the ones that we are most familiar with in 21st century computer science. Some of the history behind the creation of these databases is quite interesting. It started with an unknown researcher at IBM's San Jose, CA, research facility; a gentleman called Edgar Codd. Mr. Codd was working at IBM on hard disk research projects, but was increasingly sucked into the navigational database management systems world that would be using these hard disks. Mr. Codd became increasingly frustrated with these systems, mostly with their lack of an intuitive query interface.

Essentially, you could store data in a network/hierarchy… but how would you ever get it back out?

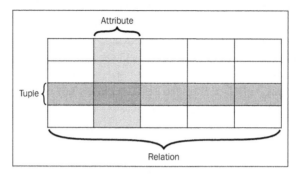

Relational database terminology

Codd wrote several papers on a different approach to database management systems that would not rely as much on linked lists of data (networks or hierarchies) but more on sets of data. He proved – using a mathematical representation called tuple calculus – that sets would be able to adhere to the same requirements that navigational database management systems were implementing. The only requirement was that there would be a proper query language that would ensure some of the consistency requirements on the database. This, then, became the inspiration for declarative query languages such as Structured Query Language, SQL. IBM's *System R* was one of the first implementations of such a system, but Software Development Laboratories, a small company founded by ex-IBM people and one illustrious Mr. Larry Ellison, actually beat IBM to the market. Their product, Oracle, never got released until a couple of years later by Relational Software, Inc., and then eventually became the flagship software product of Oracle Corporation, which we all know to day.

With relational databases came a process that all of us that have studied computer science know as **normalization**. This is the process that database modelers go through to minimize database redundancy and introduce disk storage savings, but introducing dependency. It involves splitting off data elements that appear more than once in a relational database table into their own table structures. Instead of storing the city where a person lives as a property of the person record, I would split the city into a separate table structure and store person entities in one table and city entities in another table. By doing so, we will often be creating the need to join these tables back together at query time. Depending on the cardinality of the relationship between these different tables (1:many, many:1, and many:many), this would require the introduction of a new type of table to execute these join operations: the join table, which links together two tables that would normally have a many:many cardinality.

I think it is safe to say that Relational Database Management Systems have served our industry extremely well in the past 30 years, and will probably continue to do so for a very long time to come. However, they also came with a couple of issues, which are interesting to point out as they will (again) set the stage for another generation of database management systems:

- Relational Database Systems suffer at scale. As the sets or tables of the relational systems grow longer, the query response times of the relational database systems generally get worse. Much worse. For most use cases, this was and is not necessarily a problem, but, as we all know, *size does matter*, and this deficiency certainly does harm the relational model.

- Relational Databases are quite "anti-relational". As the domains of our applications — and therefore, the relational models that represent those domains — become more complex, relational systems really start to become very difficult to work with. More specifically, join operations, where users would ask queries of the database that would pull data from a number of different sets/tables, are extremely complicated and resource intensive for the database management system. There is a true limit to the number of join operations that such a system can effectively perform, before the **join bombs** go off and the system becomes very unresponsive.

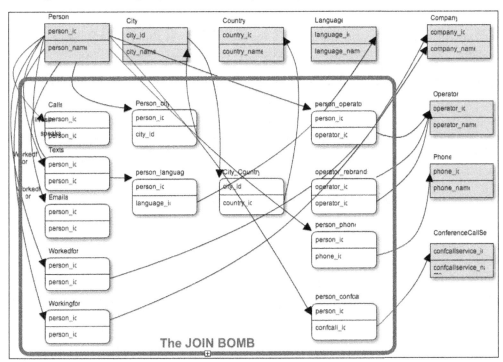

Relational database schema with explosive join tables

- Relational databases impose a schema even before we put any data into the database, and even if a schema is too rigid. Many of us work in domains where it is very difficult to apply a single database schema to all the elements of the domain that we are working with. Increasingly, we are seeing the need for a flexible type of schema that would cater to a more iterative, more agile way of developing software.

As you will see in the following sections, the next generation of database management systems is definitely not settling for what we have today, and is attempting to push innovation forward by providing solutions to some of these extremely complex problems.

NoSQL databases

The new millennium and the explosion of web content marked a new era for database management systems as well. A whole generation of new databases emerged, all categorized under the somewhat confrontational name of NOSQL databases. While it is not clear where the naming came from, it is pretty clear that it was born out of frustration with relational systems at that point in time. While most of us nowadays treat NOSQL as an acronym for Not Only SQL, the naming still remains a somewhat controversial topic among data buffs.

The basic philosophy of most NOSQL adepts, I believe, is that of the "task-oriented" database management system. It's like the old saying goes: *if all you have is a hammer, everything looks like a nail*. Well, now we have different kinds of hammers, screwdrivers, chisels, shovels, and many more tools up our sleeve to tackle our data problems. The underlying assumption then, of course, is that you are better off using the right tool for the job if you possibly can, and that for many workloads, the characteristics of the relational database may actually prove to be counterproductive. Other databases, not just SQL databases, are available now, and we can basically categorize them into four different categories:

- Key-Value stores
- Column-Family stores
- Document stores
- Graph databases

Let's get into the details of each of these stores.

Key-Value stores

Key-Value stores are probably the simplest type of task-oriented NOSQL databases. The data model of the original task at hand was probably not very complicated: Key-Value stores are mostly based on a whitepaper published by Amazon at the biennial ACM Symposium on Operating Systems Principles, called the Dynamo paper. The data model discussed in that paper is that of Amazon's shopping cart system, which was required to be always available and support extreme loads. Therefore, the underlying data model of the Key-Value store family of database management systems is indeed very simple: keys and values are aligned in an inherently schema-less data model. And indeed, scalability is typically extremely high, with clustered systems of thousands of commodity hardware machines existing at several high-end implementations such as Amazon and many others. Examples of Key-Value stores include the mentioned DynamoDB, Riak, Project Voldemort, Redis, and the newer Aerospike. The following screenshot illustrates the difference in data models:

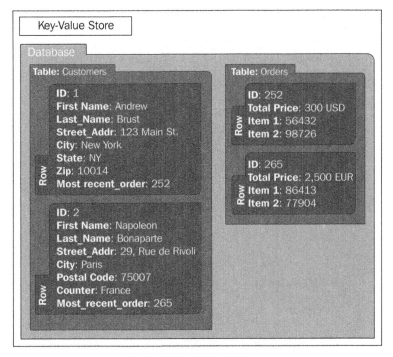

A simple Key-Value database

Column-Family stores

A Column-Family store is another example of a very task-oriented type of solution. The data model is a bit more complex than the Key-Value store, as it now includes the concept of a very wide, sparsely populated table structure that includes a number of families of columns that specify the keys for this particular table structure. Like the Dynamo system, Column-Family stores also originated from a very specific need of a very specific company (in this case, Google), who decided to roll their own solution. Google published their BigTable paper in 2006 at the **Operating Systems Design and Implementation (OSDI)** symposium. The paper not only started a lot of work within Google, but also yielded interesting open source implementations such as Apache Cassandra and Hbase. In many cases, these systems are combined with batch-oriented systems that use Map/Reduce as the processing model for advanced querying.

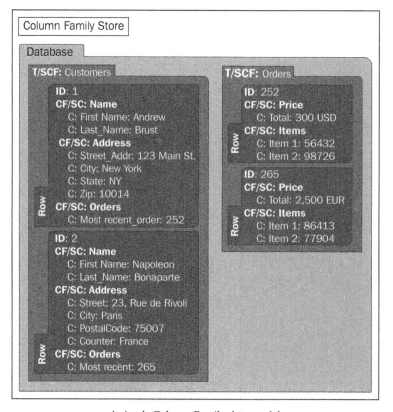

A simple Column-Family data model

Document stores

Sparked by the explosive growth of web content and applications, probably one of the most well-known and most used types of NOSQL databases are in the Document category. The key concept in a Document store, as the name suggests, is that of a semi-structured unit of information often referred to as a *document*. This can be an XML, JSON, YAML, OpenOffice, MS Office, or whatever kind of document that you may want to use, which can simply be stored and retrieved in a schema-less fashion. Examples of Document stores include the wildly popular MongoDB, and Couchbase, MarkLogic, and Virtuoso.

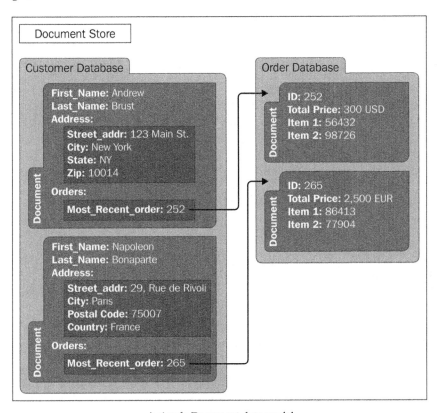

A simple Document data model

Graph databases

Last but not least, and of course the subject of most of this book, are the graph-oriented databases. They are often also categorized in the NOSQL category, but as you will see later, are inherently very different. This is not in the least the case because the task-orientation that graph databases are aiming to resolve has everything to do with graphs and graph theory that we discussed in *Chapter 1, Graphs and Graph Theory – an Introduction*. Graph databases such as Neo4j aim to provide its users with a better way to manage the complexity of the dense network of the data structure at hand. Implementations of this model are not limited to Neo4j, of course. Other closed and open source solutions such as Allegrograph, Dex, FlockDB, InfiniteGraph, OrientDB, and Sones are examples of implementations at various maturity levels.

So, now that we understand the different types of NOSQL databases, it would probably be useful to provide some general classification of this broad category of database management systems, in terms of their key characteristics. In order to do that, I am going to use a mental framework that I owe to Martin Fowler (from his book *NOSQL Distilled*) and Alistair Jones (in one of his many great talks on this subject). The reason for doing so is that both of these gentlemen and me share the viewpoint that NOSQL essentially falls into two categories, on two sides of the relational crossroads:

- On one side of the crossroads are the aggregate stores. These are the Key-Value-, Column-Family-, and Document-oriented databases, as they all share a number of characteristics:
  - They all have a fundamental data model that is based around a single, rich structure of closely-related data. In the field of software engineering called domain driven design, professionals often refer to this as an "aggregate", hence the reference to the fact that these NOSQL databases are all aggregate-oriented database management systems.
  - They are clearly optimized for use cases in which the read patterns align closely with the write patterns. What you read is what you have written. Any other use case, where you would potentially like to combine different types of data that you had previously written in separate key-value pairs / documents / rows, would require some kind of application-level processing, possibly in batch if at some serious scale.

○ They all give up one or more characteristics of the relational database model in order to benefit it in other places. Different implementations of the aggregate stores will allow you to relax your consistency/transactional requirements and will give you the benefit of enhanced (and sometimes, massive) scalability. This, obviously, is no small thing, if your problem is around scale, of course.

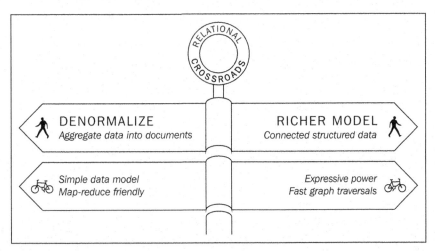

Relational crossroads, courtesy of Alistair Jones

- On the other side of the crossroads are the graph databases, such as Neo4j. One could argue that graph databases actually take relational databases:

   ○ One step further, by enhancing the data model with a more granular, more expressive method for storing data, thereby allowing much more complex questions to be asked of the database, and effectively, as we later will see, demining the join bomb.

   ○ Back to its roots, by reusing some of the original ideas of navigational databases, but of course learning from the lessons of the relational database world by reducing complexity and facilitating easy querying capabilities.

With that introduction and classification behind us, we are now ready to take a closer look at graph databases.

The Property Graph model of graph databases

The NOSQL category of graph databases, as we have seen previously, is in a class of its own. In many ways, this is because the underlying data model of graph databases—the Property Graph data model—is of a very specific nature, which we will explain a bit further.

First of all, let's define the Property Graph data model. Essentially, it means that we will be storing our data in the graph database.

A graph structure means that we will be using vertices and edges (or nodes and relationships, as we prefer to call these elements) to store data in a persistent manner. As a consequence, the graph structure enables us to:

- Represent data in a much more natural way, without some of the distortions of the relational data model
- Apply various types of graph algorithms on these structures

In short, it enables us to treat the graph nature of that data as an essential part of our capabilities. One of the key capabilities that we will find in the remainder of this book is the capability to traverse the graph—to walk on its nodes and relationships and hop from one node to the next by following the explicit pointers that connect the nodes. This capability—sometimes also referred to as *index free adjacency*, which essentially means that you can find adjacent/neighboring nodes without having to do an index lookup—is key to the performance characteristics that we will discuss in later paragraphs.

However, it is important to realize that the property graph model is not suited for all graph structures. Specifically, it is optimized for:

- **Directed graphs**: The links between nodes (also known as the relationships) have a direction.
- **Multirelational graphs**: There can be multiple relationships between two nodes that are the same. These relationships, as we will see later, will be clearly distinct and of a different type.
- Storing key-value pairs as the properties of the nodes and relationships.

In the different kinds of *properties* that can belong to the different elements of the graph structure, the most basic ones, of course, are properties assigned to vertices and edges.

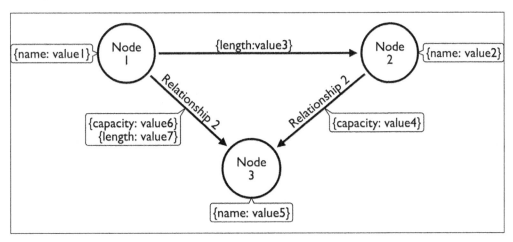

An example of a simple property graph

Let's investigate this model in a bit more detail. When looking closer at this, we find the following interesting aspects of this model:

- There is no fixed schema. The database, in and of itself, does not impose that you have to have a schema, although most software professionals will agree that having some kind of schema as you move closer to production is probably not a bad idea.

- Partly because of the schema-less nature of the database, it seems to be a very nice fit for dealing with semi-structured data. If one node or relationship has more or fewer properties, we do not have to alter the design for this; we can just deal with that difference in structure automatically and work with it in exactly the same way.

- Nodes and node properties seem to be quite easy to understand. In relational terms, one can easily compare nodes with records in a table. It's as if the property graph contains lots and lots of single-row tables, that is, the nodes of the graph. Nodes will have properties just like records/rows in a table will have fields/columns.

- Relationships are a bit different. They always have a start- and an endpoint, therefore have a direction. They cannot be dangling, but can be self-referencing (same node as start- and endpoint). But the real power lies in the fact that:

   ° **Relationships are explicit**: They are not inferred by some kind of constraint or established at query time through a join operation. They are equal citizens in the database; they have the same expressive power as the nodes representing the entities in the database.

   ° **Relationships can have properties too**: They can have values associated with them that can specify the length, capacity, or any other characteristic of that relationship. This is terribly important, and very different from anything we know from the relational world.

In Neo4j then, this data model has been enriched with a couple of key concepts that extend the core property graph model. Two concepts are important, related but different: node labels and relationship types.

Node labels

Node labels are a way of semantically categorizing the nodes in your graph. A node can have zero, one, or more labels assigned to it—similar to how you would use labels in something like your Gmail inbox. Labels are essentially a set-oriented concept in a graph structure: it allows you to easily and efficiently create subgraphs in your database, which can be useful for many different purposes. One of the most important things you can do with labels is to create some kind of typing structure or schema in your database without having to do this yourself (which is what people used to do all the time before the advent of labels in Neo4j 2.0).

Relationship types

Relationship types achieve something similar to what you do with node labels, but to relationships. The purpose of doing so, however, is mostly very different. Relationship types are mandatory properties for relationships (every relationship must have one and only one type) and will be used during complex, deep traversals across the graph, when only certain kinds of paths from node to node are deemed important by a specific query.

This should give you a good understanding of the basic data model that we will be using during the remainder of this book. Neo4j implements a very well-documented version of the property graph database, and as we will see later, is well suited for a wide variety of different use cases. Let's explore the reasons for using a graph database like Neo4j a bit more before proceeding.

Why (or why not) graph databases

By now, you should have a good understanding of what graph databases are, and how they relate to other database management systems and models. Much of the remainder of this book will be drilling into quite a bit more detail on the specifics of Neo4j as an example implementation of such a database management system. Before that, however, it makes sense to explore why these kinds of databases are of such interest to modern-day software professionals – developers, architects, project and product managers, and IT directors alike.

The fact of the matter is that there are a number of typical data problems, and database system queries are an excellent match for a graph database, and that there are a number of other types of data questions that are not specifically designed to be answered by such systems. Let's explore these for a bit and determine the characteristics of your dataset and your query patterns that will determine whether graph databases are going to be a good fit or not.

Why use a graph database?

When you are trying to solve a problem that meets any of the following descriptions, you should probably consider using a graph database such as Neo4j.

Complex queries

Complex queries are the types of questions that you want to ask of your data that are inherently composed of a number of complex join-style operations. These operations, as every database administrator knows, are very expensive operations in relational database systems, because we need to be computing the Cartesian product of the indices of the tables that we are trying to join. That may be okay for one or two joins between two or three tables in a relational database management system, but as you can easily understand, this problem becomes exponentially bigger with every table join that you add. On smaller datasets, it can become an unsolvable problem in a relational system, and this is why complex queries become problematic.

An example of such a complex query would be: find all the restaurants in a certain London neighborhood that serve Indian food, are open on Sundays, and cater for kids. In relational terms, this would mean joining up data from the **restaurant** table, the **food type** table, the **Opening hours** table, the **Caters for** table, and the zip-code table holding the London neighborhoods and then providing an answer. No doubt there are numerous other examples where you would need to do these types of complex queries; this is just a hypothetical one.

In a graph database, a join operation will never need to be performed: all we need to do is to find a starting node in the database (for example, London), usually with an index lookup, and then just use the index free adjacency characteristic and hop from one node (London) to the next (Restaurant) over its connecting relationships (Restaurant-[LOCATED_IN]->London). Every hop along this path is, in effect, the equivalent of a join operation. Relationships between nodes can therefore also be thought of as an explicitly stored representation of such a join operation.

We often refer to these types of queries as pattern matching queries. We specify a pattern (refer to the following diagram: blue connects to orange, orange connects to green, and blue connects to green), we anchor that pattern to one or more starting points, and start looking for matching occurrences of that pattern. As you can see, the graph database will be an excellent tool to spin around the anchor node and figure out whether there are matching patterns connected to it. Non-matching patterns will be ignored, and matching patterns that are not connected to the starting node will not even be considered.

This, actually, is one of the key performance characteristics of a graph database: as soon as you "grab" a starting node, the database will only explore the vicinity of that starting node and will be completely oblivious to anything that is not connected to the starting node. The key performance characteristic that follows from this is that query performance is very independent of the data set size, because in most graphs everything is not connected to everything. By the same token, as we will see later, performance will be much more dependent on the size of the result set, and this will also be one of the key things to keep in mind when putting together your persistence architecture.

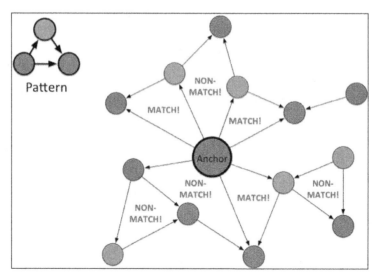

Matching patterns connected to an anchor node

In-the-clickstream queries on live data

We all know that you can implement different database queries—such as the preceding example—in different kinds of database management systems. However, in most alternative systems, these types of queries would yield terrible performance on the live database management systems, and potentially endanger the responsiveness of an entire application. The reaction of the relational database management industry, therefore, has been to make sure that these kinds of queries would be done on precalculated, preformatted data that would be specifically structured for this purpose. This means duplicating data, denormalizing data, and using techniques such as **Extract, Transform, and Load** (ETL) that are often used in Business Intelligence systems to create query-specific representations (sometimes also referred to as cubes) for the data at hand. Obviously, these are valuable techniques—the business intelligence industry would not be the billion-dollar industry that it is otherwise—but they are best suited for working with data that can be allowed to be more stale, less than up-to-date. Graph databases will allow you to answer a wider variety of these complex queries, between a web request and a web response, on data that will not have to be replicated as much, and that therefore will be updated in near real time.

Path finding queries

Another type of query that is extremely well suited for graph databases are queries where you would be looking to find out how different data elements are related to each other. In other words, finding the paths between different nodes on your graph. The problem with such queries in other database management systems is that you would actually have to understand the structure of the potential paths extremely well. You would have to be able to tell the database how to "jump" from table to table, so to speak. In a graph database, you can still do that, but typically you won't. You just tell the database to apply a graph algorithm to a starting point and an endpoint and be done with it. It's up to the database to figure out if and how these data elements would be connected to each other and return the result as a path expression for you to use in your system. The fact that you are able to delegate this to the database is extremely useful, and often leads to unexpected and valuable insights.

Obviously, the query categories mentioned above are just that: categories. You would have to apply it to any of the fields of research that we discussed in *Chapter 1, Graphs and Graph Theory – an Introduction*, to really reap the benefits. We will come back to this in later chapters.

Why not use a graph database, and what to use instead

As we discussed earlier in this chapter, the whole concept of the category of Not Only SQL databases is all about task-orientation. Use the right tool for the job. So that also must mean that there are certain use cases that graph databases are not as perfectly suited for. Being a fan of graph databases at heart, this obviously is not easy for me to admit, but it would be foolish and dishonest to claim that graph databases are the best choice for every use case. It would not be credible. So, let's briefly touch on a couple of categories of operations that you would probably want to separate from the graph database category that Neo4j belongs to.

The following operations are where I would personally not recommend using a graph database like Neo4j, or at least not in isolation.

Large, set-oriented queries

If you think back to what we discussed earlier, and think about how graph databases achieve the performance that they do in complex queries, it will also immediately follow that there are a number of cases where graph databases will still work, but will just not be as efficient. If you are trying to put together large lists of things, effectively sets, that do not require a lot of joining or require a lot of aggregation (summing, counting, averaging, and so on) on these sets, then the performance of the graph database compared to other database management systems will be not as favorable. It is clear that a graph database will be able to perform these operations, but the performance advantage will be smaller, or perhaps even negative. Set-oriented databases such as relational database management systems will most likely give just as or even more performance.

Graph global operations

As we discussed earlier, graph theory has done a lot of fascinating work on the analysis and understanding of graphs in their entirety. Finding clusters of nodes, discovering unknown patterns of relationships between nodes, and defining centrality and/or in-betweenness of specific graph components are extremely interesting and wonderful concepts, but they are very different concepts from the ones that graph databases excel at. These concepts are looking at the graph in its entirety, and we refer to them as graph global operations. While graph databases are extremely powerful at answering "graph local" questions, there is an entire category of graph tools (often referred to as graph processing engines or graph compute engines) that look at the graph global problems.

Many of these tools serve an extremely specific purpose, and even use specific hardware and software (usually using lots of memory and CPU horsepower) to achieve their tasks, and typically are part of a very different side of the IT architecture. Graph processing is typically done in batches, in the background, over the course of several hours/days/weeks and would typically not be well placed between a web request and a web response. It's a very different kind of ball game.

Simple, aggregate-oriented queries

We mentioned that graphs and graph database management systems are great for complex queries—things that would make your relational system choke. As a consequence, simple queries, where write patterns and read patterns align to the aggregates that we are trying to store, are typically served quite inefficiently in a graph, and would be more efficiently handled by an aggregate-oriented Key-Value or Document store. If complexity is low, the advantage of using a graph database system will be lower too.

Hopefully, this gives you a better view of the things that graph databases are good and not so good at.

Test questions

Q1. Which other category of databases bears the most resemblance to graph databases?

1. Navigational databases.
2. Relational Databases.
3. Column-Family stores.
4. None; graph databases are unique.

Q2. The data model of graph databases is often described as the proprietary graph data model, containing nodes, relationships, and proprietary elements.

1. True.
2. False.

Q3. Simple, aggregate-oriented queries yielding a list of things are a great application for a graph database.

1. True.
2. False.

Summary

In this chapter, we wanted to give you a bit of context before diving into the wonderful world of graph databases headfirst. It's a good idea, from an architect's point of view, to understand how graph database management systems like Neo4j came about, what problems they are trying to solve, what they are good at, and what they are perhaps less well suited for.

With that in mind, we are now ready to get our hands dirty, and start with actually playing around with Neo4j, the world's leading graph database.

3
Getting Started with Neo4j

In this chapter, we will be taking a much closer look at the real subject of this book, that is, learning Neo4j—the world's leading graph database. In this chapter, we will be going through and familiarizing ourselves with the database management system so that we can start using it in the following chapters with real-world models and use cases.

We will discuss the following topics in this chapter:

- Key concepts and characteristics of Neo4j
- Neo4j's sweet spot use cases
- Neo4j's licensing model
- Installing Neo4j
- Using Neo4j in the cloud

Let's start with the first topic straightaway.

Neo4j – key concepts and characteristics

Before we dive into the details of Neo4j, let's take a look at some of the key characteristics of Neo4j specifically as a graph database management system. Hopefully, this will immediately point out and help you get to grips with some of the key strengths as well.

Built for graphs, from the ground up

Like many open source projects and many open source NoSQL database management systems, Neo4j too came into existence for very specific reasons. *Scratching the itch*, as this is sometimes called. Grassroots developers who want to solve a problem and are struggling to do so with traditional technology stacks, decide to take a radical, new-found approach. That's what the Neo4j founders did early on in the 21st century — they built something to solve a problem for a particular media company in order to better manage media assets.

In the early days, Neo4j was not a full-on graph database management system — it was more like a **graph library** that people could use in their code to deal with connected data structures in an easier way. It was sitting on top of traditional, MySQL (and other) relational database management systems and was much more focused on creating a graph abstraction layer for developers than anything else. Clearly, this was not enough. After a while, the open source project took a radical decision to move away from the MySQL infrastructure and to build a graph store from the ground up. The key thing here is *from the ground up*. The entire infrastructure, including low-level components such as the binary file layout of the graph database store files, is optimized for dealing with graph data. This is important in many ways, as it will be the basis for many of the speed and other improvements that Neo4j will display versus other database management systems.

We don't need to understand the details of this file structure for the basis of this book — but suffice to say that it is a native, graph-oriented storage format that is tuned for this particular workload. That, dear reader, makes a big difference.

Transactional, ACID-compliant database

Neo4j prides itself in being an ACID-compliant database. To explain this further, it's probably useful to go back to what ACID really means. Basically, the acronym is one of the oldest summaries of four goals that many database management systems strive for, and they are shown in the following figure:

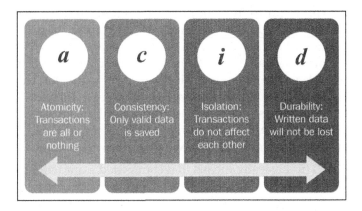

- **Atomicity**: This means that changes in the database must follow an *all or nothing* rule. Transactions are said to be "atomic" if one part of the transaction fails, then the consequence would be that the entire transaction is rolled back.

- **Consistency**: This means that only consistent or "valid" data will be allowed to be entered into the database. In relational terminology, this often means that the *schema* of the database has to be applied and maintained at all times. The main consistency requirement in Neo4j is actually that the graph relationships must have a start and an end node. Relationships cannot be dangling. Aside from this, however, the consistency rules in Neo4j will obviously be much looser, as Neo4j implements the concept of an "optional" schema.

The optional schema of Neo4j is really interesting: the idea being that it is actually incredibly useful to have a schema-free database when you are still at the beginning of your development cycles. As you are refining your knowledge about the domain and its requirements, your data model will just grow with you — free of any requirements to pre-impose a schema on your iterations. However, as you move closer to production, schema — and therefore consistency — can be really useful. At that point, system administrators and business owners alike will want to have more checks and balances around data quality, and the C in ACID will become more important. Neo4j fully supports both approaches, which is tremendously useful in today's agile development methodologies.

- **Isolation**: This requires that multiple transactions that are executed in parallel on the same database instance would not impact each other. The transactions need to take their due course, irrespective of what is happening in the system at the same time. One of the important ways that this is used is in the example where one transaction is writing to the database and another is reading from it. In an **isolated** database, the read transaction cannot know about the write that is occurring "next to" it until the transaction of the write operation is complete and fully committed. As long as the *write* operation is not committed, the *read* operation will have to work with the "old" data.

- **Durability**: This basically means that committed transactions cannot just disappear and be lost. Persisted storage and transaction commit logs that are forced to be written to disk—even when the actual data structures have not been updated yet—ensure this quality in most database systems and also in Neo4j.

The summary of all this is probably that Neo4j, really, has been designed from the ground up to be a true multipurpose database-style solution. It shares many of the qualities of a traditional relational database management system that we know today—it just uses a radically different data model that is well suited for densely connected use cases.

Made for Online Transaction Processing

The mentioned characteristics help with systems where you really need to be returning data from the database management system in an online system environment. This means that the queries that you want to ask the database management system would need to be answered in the timespan between a web request and a web response. In other words, in milliseconds—not seconds, let alone minutes.

This characteristic is not required of every database management system. Many systems actually only need to reply to requests that are first fired off and then require an answer many hours later. In the world of relational database systems, we call these analytical systems. We refer to the difference between the two types of systems as the difference between **Online Transaction Processing** (OLTP) and **Online Analytical Processing** (OLAP). There's a significant difference between the two—from a conceptual as well as from a technical perspective. So let's compare the two in the following table:

	Online Transaction Processing (Operational System)	Online Analytical Processing (Analytical System, also known as the data warehouse)
Source of data	Operational data; OLTPs are the original source of the data	Consolidation data; OLAP data comes from the various OLTP databases
Purpose of data	To control and run fundamental business tasks	To help with planning, problem solving, and decision support
What the data provides	Reveals a snapshot of ongoing business processes	Multidimensional views of various kinds of business activities
Inserts and updates	Short and fast inserts and updates initiated by end users	Periodic long-running batch jobs refresh the data
Queries	Relatively standardized and simple queries returning relatively few records	Often complex queries involving aggregations
Processing speed	Typically very fast	Depends on the amount of data involved; batch data refreshes and complex queries may take many hours
Space requirements	Can be relatively small if historical data is archived	Larger due to the existence of aggregation structures and history data; requires more indexes than OLTP
Database design	Highly normalized with many tables	Typically de-normalized with fewer tables; use of star and/or snowflake schemas
Backup and recovery	Backs up religiously; operational data is critical to run the business, data loss is likely to entail significant monetary loss and legal liability	Instead of regular backups, some environments may consider simply reloading the OLTP data as a recovery method

At the time of writing this, Neo4j is clearly in the OLTP side of the database ecosystem. That does not mean that you cannot do any analytical tasks with Neo4j. In fact, some analytical tasks in the relational world are far more efficiently run on a graph database (see the sweet spot query section that follows later), but it is not optimized for it. Typical Neo4j implementation recommendations would also suggest that you put aside a separate Neo4j instance for these analytical workloads so that it would not impact your production OLTP queries. In the future, Neo Technology plans to make further enhancements to Neo4j that make it even more suited for OLAP tasks.

Designed for scalability

In order to deal with the OLTP workload, Neo4j obviously needs to be able to support critical scalability, high availability, and fault-tolerance requirements. Creating clusters of database server instances that work together to achieve the goals stated before typically solves this problem. Neo4j's Enterprise Edition, therefore, features a clustering solution that has been proven to support even the most challenging workloads.

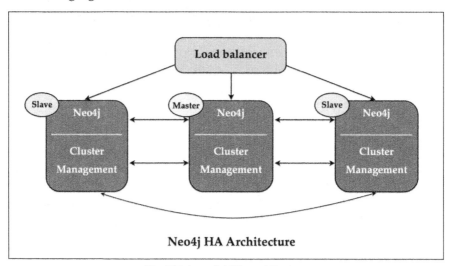

Neo4j high availability architecture

As you can see from the preceding diagram, the Neo4j clustering solution is a master-slave clustering solution. In a particular cluster, each server instance of the cluster will perform the following steps:

- Hold the entire dataset of the database. All servers hold the same data and therefore can respond to all query requests.

- Comply with a master-slave consistency scheme. This means that, in case of potential conflicting data in the database, the **Master** server instance will decide what would be right data to keep and persist. If at some point, the cluster would lose its master, the remaining cluster member instances would run a master election algorithm (in Neo4j's case, based on Paxos) that allows them to quickly choose a new master.

- The server should be optimized to deal with a particular subset of the queries that hit the cluster. For example, the load balancer would be configured in such a way that specific types of queries (for example, write queries versus read queries, queries for a specific region/continent, and queries from a specific application) would be directed to a specific cluster member. The advantage of doing so is that this will allow Neo4j to optimize its caching content and use a concept that we sometimes refer to as a "sharded cache". This means that the cluster members may in fact be holding the same dataset in their database store files, but in memory, in the cache, they will hold very different parts of the graph. Similar to any database management system, queries served up from a cache will be much faster. So, we want to try and optimize the cluster for this. If by some twist of fate the queries don't end up on the right instance, then that does not mean that the application will stop functioning. It will just not respond from cache, and therefore respond a bit slower.

Neo4j's clustering solution allows you to provide the following features:

- **Horizontal scalability**: This is provided by adding more machines to the cluster and distributing the load over the cluster members
- **Vertical scalability**: This is provided by adding more horsepower (CPU, memory, disks, and so on) to the machines that are the cluster members

This covers 99 percent of all use cases — the references of Neo Technology speak for itself.

A declarative query language – Cypher

One of the defining features of the Neo4j graph database product today is its wonderful query language, called Cypher. Cypher is a declarative, pattern-matching query language that makes graph database management systems understandable and workable for any database user — even the less technical ones.

The key characteristic of Cypher is, in my opinion, that it is a **declarative** language, opposed to other imperative query languages that have existed for quite some time. Why is this so important? Here are your answers:

- Declarative languages allow you to state what you're looking for, declare the pattern that you would like to see retrieved, and then let the database worry about how to go about retrieving that data.

  In an imperative (query) language, you would have to *tell* the database specifically what to do to get to the data and retrieve it.

- Declarative languages separate the concern of stating the problem, from solving it. This allows greater readability of the queries that you write, which is important as people tend to read their database queries more often than they write them. This piece of your software will therefore become more readable and shareable with others, and long term maintenance of that easy-to-read query becomes so much easier.

- Declarative languages will allow the database to use the information that it holds about the nature and structure of the data to answer your question more efficiently. Essentially, it allows query optimizations that you would never have known of or thought about in an imperative approach. Therefore, declarative languages can be faster — at least over time as the optimization algorithms mature.

- Declarative languages are great for adhoc querying of your database, without you having to write complex software routines to do so.

Part of the reason why I feel that Cypher is such an important part of Neo4j is that we know that declarative languages, especially in the database management systems world, are critical to mass adoption. Most application developers do not want to be worrying about the nitty gritty of how to best interact with their data. They want to focus on the business logic and the data *should just be there* when I want it, as I want it. This is exactly how relational database systems evolved in the seventies (refer to *Chapter 2, Graph Databases – Overview*). It is highly likely that we will be seeing a similar evolution in the graph database management system space. Cypher, therefore, is in a unique position and makes it so much easier to work with the database. It is already an incredible tool today, and it will only become better.

Sweet spot use cases of Neo4j

Like with many software engineering tools, Neo4j too has its sweet spot use cases — specific types of uses that the tool really shines and adds a lot of value to your process. Many tools can do many things and so can Neo4j, but only a few things can be done really well by a certain tool. We have addressed some of this already in the previous chapter. However, to summarize specifically for the Neo4j software package, I believe that there are two particular types of cases — featuring two specific types of database queries — where the tool really excels.

Complex, join-intensive queries

We discussed in the previous chapter how relational database management systems suffer from significant drawbacks, as they have to deal with more and more complex data models. Asking these kinds of questions of a relational database requires the database engine to calculate the Cartesian product of the full indices on the tables involved in the query. That computation can take a very long time on larger datasets, or if more than two tables are involved.

Graph database management systems do not suffer from these problems. The join operations are effectively precalculated and explicitly persisted in the database based on the relationships that connect nodes together. Therefore, joining data becomes as simple as hopping from one node to another—effectively as simple as following a pointer. These complex questions that are so difficult to ask in a relational world are extremely simple, efficient, and fast in a graph structure.

Path finding queries

Many users of Neo4j use the graph structure of their data to find out whether there are useful paths between different nodes on the network. *Useful* in this phrase is probably the operative word; they are looking for specific paths on the network to:

- See whether the path actually exists. Are there any connections between two data elements, and if so what does that connectivity look like?

- Look for the optimal path. Which path between two things has the lowest "cost?"

- Look for the variability of the path if a certain component of the path changes. What happens to the path if the properties of a node or relationship change?

Both of these sweet spot use cases share a couple of important characteristics:

- They are "graph local" and they have one or more fixed starting point(s), or "anchor", in the graph from where the graph database engine can start traversing out

- They are performed "in the clickstream", and therefore performed on near-real-time data

Let's now switch to another key element of Neo4j's success as a graph database management system: the fact that it is an open source solution.

Committed to open source

One of the key things that we have seen happening in Enterprise information technology, is the true and massive adoption of open source technologies for many of its business-critical applications. This has been an evolution that has lasted a decade at least, starting with peripheral systems such as web servers (in the days when web servers were still considered to be serving static web pages), but gradually evolving to mission critical operating systems, content management applications, CRM systems and databases such as Neo4j.

There are many interesting aspects to open source software, but some of the most often quoted are listed as follows:

*   **Lower chance of vendor lock-in**: Since the code is readily available, the user of the software could also read the code themselves and potentially understand how to work with it (and extend it, or fix it, or audit it, and so on) independently of the vendor.

*   **Better security**: As the code is undergoing public scrutiny and because there is no way for a developer to implement "security through obscurity" (for example by using a proprietary algorithm that no one knows and would have to reverse engineer), open source software systems should be intrinsically more secure.

*   **Easier support and troubleshooting**: As both the vendor and the customer have access to the source code, it should be easier to exchange detailed, debug-level information about the running system and make it easier to pinpoint problems.

*   **More innovation through extensibility**: By exposing source code, many people left and right will start playing with the software—even without the original author knowing that this is going on. This typically causes these "community contributors" to solve problems that they encounter with the product, in their specific use case, and it leads to faster innovation and extensibility of the solution.

*   **Supporting (fundamental and applied) research**: Open source solutions —even the ones equipped with enterprise commercial features such as Neo4j—usually allow researchers to use the software for free. Most researchers also published their work as open source code. So, it's a two-way street.

*   **Cheaper**: open source software tends to use "fair" licensing models. You only need to pay if you derive value from the software and are not able to contribute your code. This not only allows cheaper evaluation of the software in the start of the process—hopefully avoiding unused shelfware —but also allows enterprises to start with limited investments and grow gradually as the use expands.

I believe that all is true for Neo4j. Let's look at the different parameter axes that determine the license model. Three parameters are important, which are explained in the following sections.

The features

Neo4j offers different feature sets for different editions of the graph database management system:

- **Community Edition**: This is the basic, fully functional, high-performance graph database.
- **Enterprise Edition**: This adds a number of typical Enterprise features to the Community Edition: clustering (for high availability and load balancing), advanced monitoring, advanced caching, and online backups. Neo Technology has a number of additional features lined up on the Enterprise Edition roadmap.

Most users of Neo4j start off with the Community Edition, but then deploy into production on the Enterprise Edition.

The support

Different support channels exist for Neo4j's different editions:

- The Community Edition offers "community support". This means that you are welcome to ask questions and seek support on the public forums (Google group, Stack Overflow, Twitter, and other channels). However, note the following points:
  - The responses will always need to be publicized (cannot be private)
  - The response will not be guaranteed or timed

  Neo Technology does sponsor a significant team of top-notch engineers to help the community users, but at the end of the day, this formula does have its limitations.

- The Enterprise Edition offers a professional grade support team that is available 24/7, follows the sun, and has different prioritization levels with guaranteed response times. At the time of writing this, Neo Technology also offers direct access to its engineers that write the product so that customers can literally get first-hand information and help from the people that build Neo4j themselves.

The support program for Neo4j is typically something that is most needed at the beginning of the process (as that is when the development teams have most questions about the new technology that they are using), but it is often only sought at the end of a development cycle.

The license conditions

For the slightly more complicated bit, Neo Technology has chosen very specific licensing terms for Neo4j, which may seem a tad complicated but actually really supports the following goals:

- Promoting open source software
- Promoting community development of Neo4j
- Assuring the long-term viability of the Neo4j project by providing for a revenue stream.

This is achieved in the following ways:

- The Community Edition uses the GNU Public License Version 3 (GPLv3) as its licensing terms. This means that you may copy, distribute, and modify the software as long as you track changes/dates of in source files and keep modifications under GPL. You can distribute your application using a GPL library commercially, but you must also provide the source code. It is therefore a very viral license and requires you to open source your code—but only if your code directly interfaces with the Neo4j code through the Java API. If you are using the REST API, then there are little or no contamination effects and you can just use Neo4j at will.

- The Enterprise Edition uses a so-called dual license model. This means that users of the Neo4j Enterprise Edition can choose one of two options:

    ○ Either they adhere to the Affero GNU Public License Version 3 (AGPLv3), which is sometimes also referred to as the "GPL for the web".

The AGPL license differs from the other GNU licenses in that it was built for network software. Similar conditions apply as to the GPL; however, it is even more "viral" in the sense that it requires you to open source your code not only when you link your code on the same machine (through Neo4j's Java API), but also if you interface with Neo4j over the network (through Neo4j's REST API). So, this means that if you use Neo4j's Enterprise Edition for free, you have to open source your code.

- Get a **Neo Technology Commercial License** (**NTCL**). This license is a typical commercial subscription license agreement, which gives you the right to use Neo4j Enterprise Edition for a certain period of time, on a certain number of machines/instances.

All of the mentioned points are summarized in the following figure:

	Community Edition	Enterprise Edition	
License	GPL: • Open Source • Free to use via REST API if Commercial • Requirement to open source derivative works if using JAVA API	AGPL • Open Source • Free to use if derivative works are also open sourced	Neo Technology Commercial License (NTCL) • Open Source
Features	High Performance Graph Database, native language bindings and web frameworks integration	High Performance Graph Database native language bindings and web frameworks integration	
		Neo4j Web Management Console advanced monitoring	
		High Availability & Massive Read Scaling via Clustering Online failover & backups Advanced Caching	
Support Services	Online Community Support for **General Interest** questions	Online Community Support for **General Interest** questions	Email & Phone, 7×24 support for **Customer Specific** questions
Annual Subscription	Free	Free	Different programs and Bundles available

An overview of the Neo4j license

As indicated in the preceding figure, Neo Technology offers a number of different annual commercial subscription options, depending on the number of instances that you will deploy, the type of company you are (startup, mid-sized corporation, or large corporation), the legal contract requirements of the agreement, and the support contract. For more information on the specifics of these bundles—which change regularly—you can contact sales@neotechnology.com.

With that, we have wrapped up this section and will now proceed to getting our hands dirty with Neo4j on the different platforms available.

Installing Neo4j

In this section, we will take you through the first couple of steps that you need to take to get started with Neo4j. These steps are quite a bit different on different platforms, therefore we will be going through the different options one by one and looking at the common steps. For most, this will be a simple step—but it's an important one that we cannot afford to skip.

Installing Neo4j on Windows

Like on any platform, installing Neo4j starts with downloading the latest version from the Neo4j website: `http://www.Neo4j.org/download` is where the most recent versions can be found.

 Currently, interfacing with Neo4j is done best with a webkit-based browser, such as Chrome (which is the browser that we will be using for this section), on all platforms.

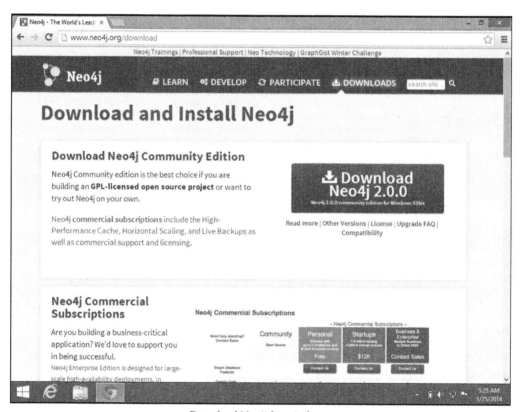

Download Neo4j for windows

Neo4j Community Edition offers an excellent starting point for your exploration of the Neo4j ecosystem, and on Windows, the download process initiated provides you with an executable Windows installer that gives you the smoothest installation experience.

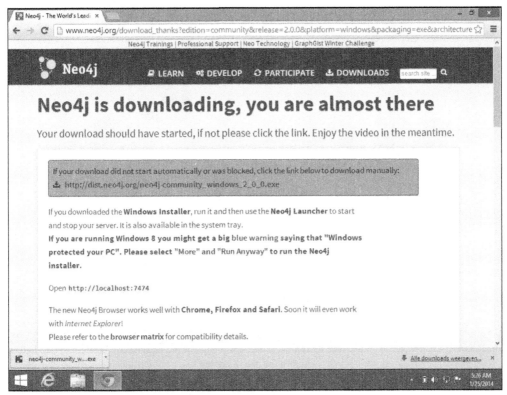

The downloaded Neo4j installer

Once Neo4j is downloaded, the Windows installer provides you with all the necessary options to install Neo4j smoothly and efficiently.

Accept the Neo4j license

After you accept the license agreement, the setup wizard will allow you to immediately run the software:

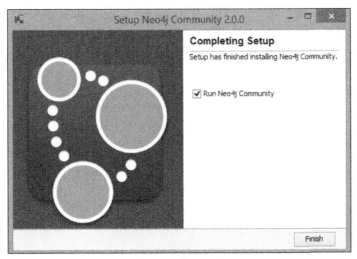

Complete installation of Neo4j

The following screenshot shows that Neo4j is initiated when you finish the setup instructions:

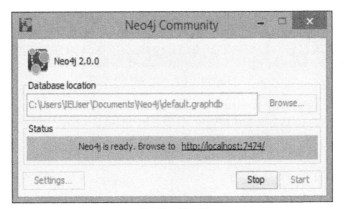

Starting Neo4j

Once Neo4j is running, you can immediately access the server with the Neo4j browser:

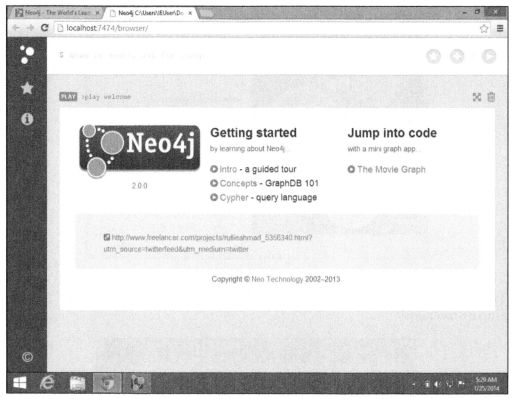

Accessing the Neo4j browser

Accessing the Neo4j server binaries or any of the accompanying tools can be done from the filesystem, which would typically be in the `C:\Program Files\Neo4j Community` directory.

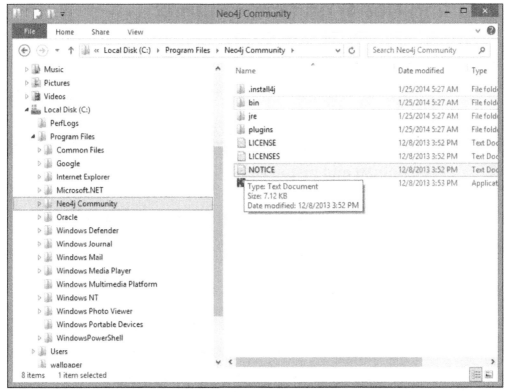

The Neo4j file structure on Windows

With that, we now have a running server on our Microsoft Windows machine and we are ready to start working with it. We will do so right after we explore some of the other remaining platforms.

Installing Neo4j on Mac or Linux

Downloading Neo4j for the Mac or Linux platforms is of course very similar. The Neo4j website will automatically detect your platform and start downloading the appropriate version.

Download Neo4j for OS X/Linux

The only major difference in the download process, however, is in the fact that the Java runtime is not bundled with the downloaded files. On Windows, as we saw previously, there is no need to install anything but the Neo4j installer. On Mac OS X and Linux, however, you need to make sure that Java 7 is installed and configured to be used as the default Java Virtual Machine. In this book, we will assume that you know how to do this—if not, you may want to search for *Neo4j java 7 OS X* using a browser and you will find the required articles to solve this.

I will be using OS X as my home operating system, but the process should be almost identical on Linux.

First, you start with downloading the file that contains Neo4j.

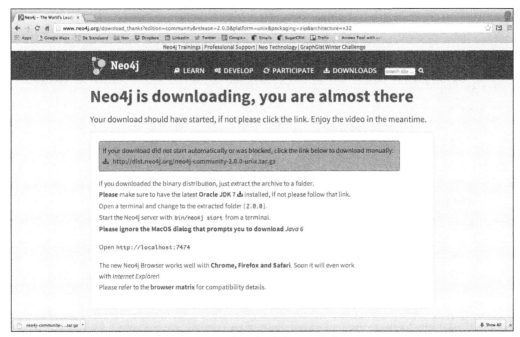

Neo4j is downloaded as a tarball

Next, you just need to uncompress the download in a location of your preference. You can do that with a graphical tool (just double-clicking the compressed file) or by using the command-line utility that ships with your OS X or Linux distribution. In any case, you will get a file structure similar to the one shown in the following screenshot:

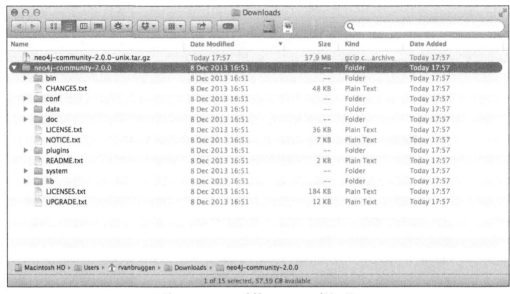

The uncompressed file structure of Neo4j

Next, you should open a terminal in the directory highlighted in the preceding screenshot. By running a simple command (`bin/neo4j start`), you will start Neo4j at the default location:

```
Sat Jan 25, 18:00:02 $ pwd
/Users/rvanbruggen/Downloads/neo4j-community-2.0.0
Sat Jan 25, 18:00:09 $
Sat Jan 25, 18:00:10 $ bin/neo4j start
Using additional JVM arguments:  -server -XX:+DisableExplicitGC -Dorg.neo4j.server.proper
ties=conf/neo4j-server.properties -Djava.util.logging.config.file=conf/logging.properties
 -Dlog4j.configuration=file:conf/log4j.properties -XX:+UseConcMarkSweepGC -XX:+CMSClassUn
loadingEnabled
Starting Neo4j Server...WARNING: not changing user
process [15549]... waiting for server to be ready.... OK.
http://localhost:7474/ is ready.
Sat Jan 25, 18:00:16 $
```

Starting Neo4j from the command line

Accessing Neo4j's browser is completely analogous to the Windows installation illustrated previously; all you need to do is point your browser to `http://localhost:7474` and you should be good to go.

Starting the Neo4j browser

The default installation of Neo4j also comes with some tutorials and a simple dataset that you can play around with. Hopefully, this is enough to get you going; it certainly is enough for this chapter of the book.

Using Neo4j in a cloud environment

In this section, we are going to address a third and alternative way of getting started with the Neo4j graph database management system, that is, by using a cloud solution. As it turns out, you can try out the power of the database solution without even having to go through the previously mentioned steps of installing the product on an operating system of your own. You can just use a "graph as a service" solution; there are multiple providers out there. At the time of writing this, you can use solutions from the following:

- GrapheneDB.com
- Heroku
- GraphAlchemist
- ElastX
- Of course, a "roll your own" solution on Amazon Web Services would work just as nicely

Therefore, we are going to explain and illustrate some of the principles of a cloud-based deployment model and how you can use it to get started. To do so, we will be using the GrapheneDB platform—probably one of the most simple, elegant, and powerful solutions out there.

Getting started with the cloud platform consists of a few simple steps:

1. Register with GrapheneDB. This is easy enough, as they offer a free tier to test out the solution and get started.

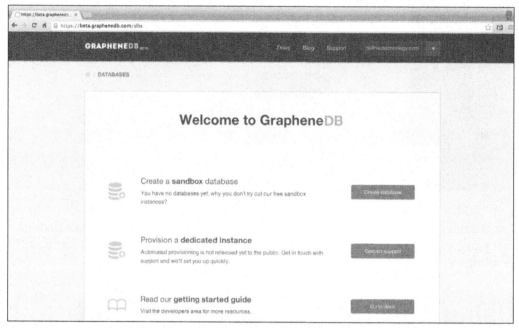

Starting with GrapheneDB

2. Create a database instance. This is the equivalent of starting up a Neo4j server, but just not on your own server hardware.

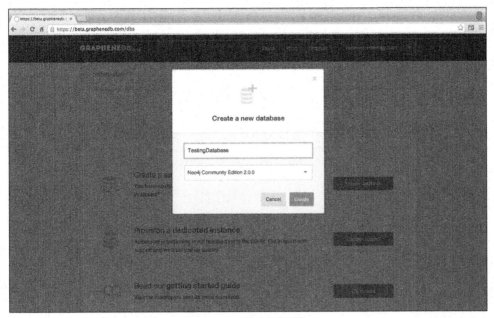

Create a new Neo4j database

3. Once the database has been created, we can start using it. The **Admin** panel shows us the way, and gives immediate access to this particular Neo4j instance's browser interface.

Start using a Neo4j database

4. In that browser interface, we can do everything we would normally be able to do, except for the fact that this interface is protected by an implicit username/ password combination. Running a few queries immediately feels familiar; the experience is nearly identical to that of running a local database server.

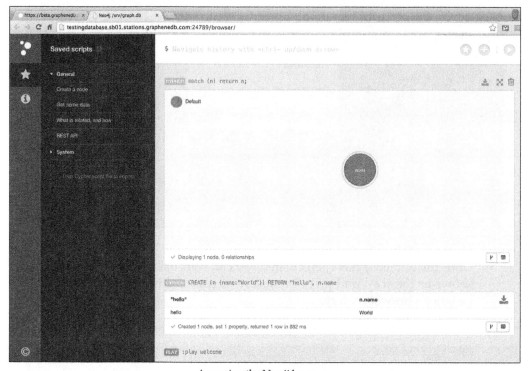

Accessing the Neo4j browser

One of the few differences that you will notice is the way you access the REST interface—if you are using specific language bindings, for example. These configurations are very specific and need to be taken into account:

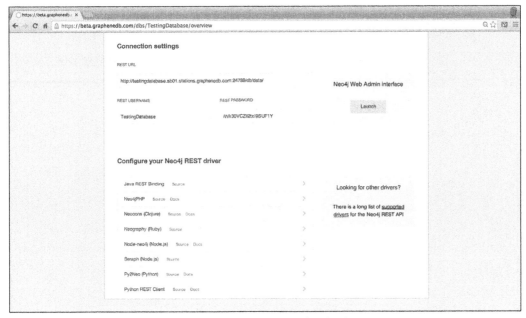

REST connection settings for Neo4j

5. Finally, if you want to administer your cloud-based Neo4j system, you can access the following web page to perform exports and imports of your database, for example. The latter is of course interesting and important, as it allows you to create a database on your local machine and then transfer the zipped `graph.db` directory onto the Neo4j instance at `http://www.graphenedb.com/`.

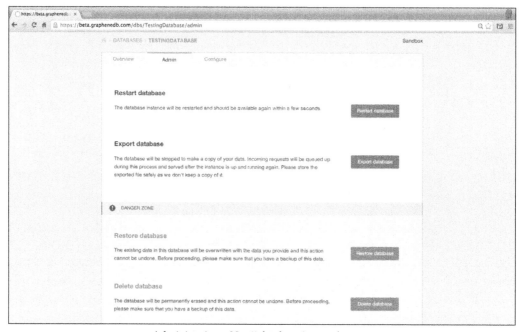

Administering a Neo4j database import/export

I hope this gives you a good overview of how you can get started with Neo4j with a provider such as GrapheneDB. It definitely flattens the learning curve even further and makes it easier for people to start using Neo4j in real production environments.

Test Questions

Q1. Neo4j is an ACID database.

1. True.
2. False.

Q2. The Enterprise Edition of Neo4j is available in which of the following license formats:

1. A closed-source, proprietary license, to be purchased from Neo Technology.
2. An open source license, the Apache 2 License.
3. An open source license, the Affero GNU Public license.
4. A dual license—either the open source Affero GNU Public license or the open source Neo Technology Commercial License to be purchased from Neo Technology.

Q3. Neo4j is only available on Linux/Unix/OS X based systems.

1. True.
2. False.

Summary

In this chapter, we discussed the background material for Neo4j specifically, as the world's leading graph database and the topic of the rest of this book. This included an overview of Neo4j's specific implementation of the graph database concepts, its sweet spot use cases, its licensing model, and its installation and deployment considerations. This should give us the required background to get going with the hands-on part of this book. This is what we will start to address now, and the next chapter will help you to model your data in the right way that is fit for Neo4j.

4
Modeling Data for Neo4j

In this chapter, we will get started with some graph database modeling in Neo4j. As this type of modeling can be quite different from what we are typically used to with our relational database backgrounds, we will start by explaining the fundamental constructs first and then explore some recommended approaches.

We will cover the following topics in this chapter:

- Modeling principles and how-to's
- Modeling pitfalls and best practices

The four fundamental data constructs

As you may already know by now, graph theory gives us many different graphs to work with. Graphs come in many different shapes and sizes, and therefore, Neo4j needed to choose a very specific type of data structure that is flexible enough to support the versatility required by real-world datasets. This is why the underlying data model of Neo4j, the labeled property graph, is one of the most generic and versatile of all graph models.

This graph data model gives us four different fundamental building blocks to structure and store our data. Let's go through them:

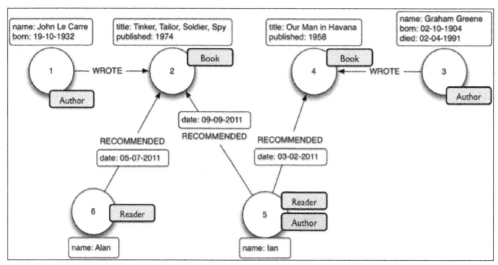

The labeled property graph model

- **Nodes**: These are typically used to store entity information. In the preceding example, these are the individual books, readers, and authors that are present in the library data model.

- **Relationships**: These are used to connect nodes to one another explicitly and therefore provide a means of structuring your entities. They are the equivalent of an explicitly stored, and therefore pre-calculated, join-like operation in a relational database management system. As we have seen in the previous chapters, joins are no longer a query-time operation – they are as simple as the traversal of a relationship connecting two nodes. Relationships always have a type, a start- *and* an end-node, and a direction. They can be self-referencing/looping and can never be dangling (missing start- or end-node).

- **Properties**: Both nodes and relationships are containers for properties, which are effectively name/value pairs. In the case of the nodes, this is very intuitive. Just like a record in the relational database world has one or more fields or attributes, so can the node have one or more properties. Less intuitive is the fact that relationships can have properties too. These are used to further qualify the strength or quality of a relationship and can be used during queries/traversals to evaluate the patterns that we are looking for.

- **Labels**: This was a fundamental data model construct that was added to Neo4j with Version 2.0 at the end of 2013. Labels are a means to quickly and efficiently create subgraphs. By assigning labels to nodes, Neo4j makes the data model of most users a lot simpler. There is no longer a need to work with a *type* property on the nodes, or a need to connect nodes to *definition* nodes that provide meta-information about the graph. Neo4j now does this out of the box—and this is a huge asset, now and for the future. At the time of writing this book, labels are primarily used for indexing and some limited schema constraints. However, in future, it is likely that the structural understanding that labels provide about the data stored in the graph will be used for other purposes such as additional schema, security, graph sharding/distribution—and perhaps others.

With these four data constructs, we can now start working with Neo4j.

How to start modeling for graph databases

In this section, we will spend some time going through what a graph database model is. Specifically, we would like to clarify a common misunderstanding that originates from our habitual relational database system knowledge.

What we know – ER diagrams and relational schemas

In a relational system, we have been taught to start out modeling with an Entity-Relationship diagram. Using these techniques, we can start from a problem/domain description (what we call a user story in today's agile development methodologies) and extract the meaningful entities and relationships. We will come back to this later, but essentially, we usually find that from such a domain description, we can:

- Extract the entities by looking at the nouns of the description
- Extract the properties by looking at the adjectives of the description
- Extract the relationship by looking at the operating verbs in the description

These are, of course, generic guidelines that will need to be tried and tested on every domain individually to make sure that it is an appropriate fit. However, for now, let's look at the following diagram:

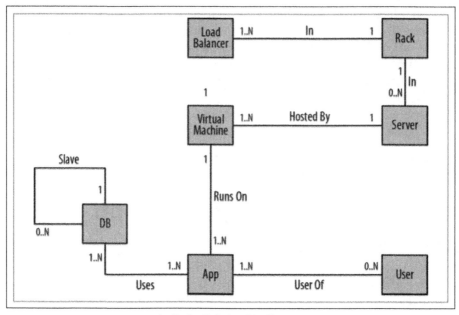

An Entity-Relationship diagram

As you can see from the preceding figure, ER diagrams have the advantage of at least attempting to capture the business domain in a real-world model. However, they suffer from quite a few disadvantages too. Despite being visually very similar to graph visualizations, ER diagrams immediately demonstrate the shortcomings of the relational model to capture a rich domain. Although they allow relationships to be named (something that graph databases fully embrace, but relational stores do not), ER diagrams allow only single, undirected, named but otherwise unqualified relationships between entities. In this respect, the relational model is a poor fit for real-world domains where relationships between entities are numerous, semantically rich, and diverse. The labeled property graph, as we have seen previously, allows for a much richer description of the domain, specifically with regard to the relationships between the entities—which will be multiple, directed, and qualified through properties.

The problem of relational ER modeling becomes even worse when we take the ER diagram to an actual system and are faced with serious limitations. Let's take a look at how one of the relational model's fundamental problems becomes apparent when we take the diagram to a test in a real-world implementation.

Introducing complexity through join tables

Let's take the model, which was described previously, to the database administrator for an actual implementation. What happens then is that in this implementation, the relational model inherently causes complexity. What you can see in the following diagram is that for every relationship where we can have *n-n* combinations, we actually need to introduce something that links the two tables together. This is what we call a join table, and this will be used by every query that requests a combination of the *n-n* entities.

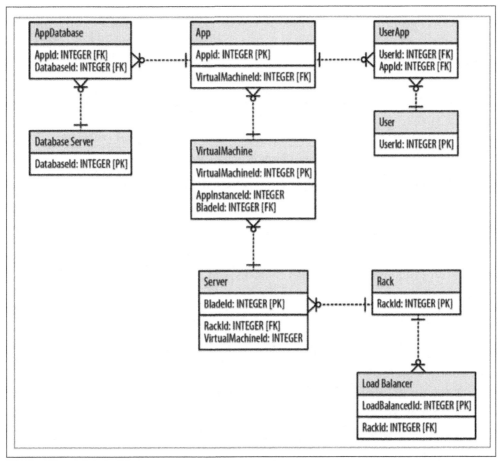

The database schema

In the previous example, we introduced the **AppDatabase** table to link applications to database servers and the **UserApp** table to link **Users** to **Applications**. These join tables are only necessary to deal with the shortcomings of the relational model, and they complicate our lives as database administrators and application developers. They introduce unwanted complexity.

A graph model – a simple, high-fidelity model of reality

Let's take a quick look at how we can avoid the complexity mentioned previously in the graph world. In the following figure, you will find the graph model and the relational model side by side:

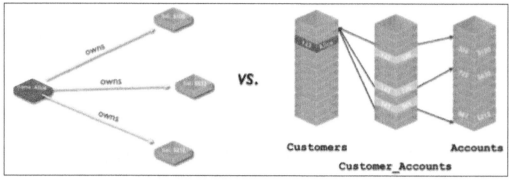

The relational model versus the graph model

On the right-hand side of the image, you will see the three tables in the relational model:

- A **customers** table with a number of customer records
- An **Accounts** table with a number of accounts of these customers
- A typical join table that links customers to accounts

What is important here is the implication of this construction: every single time we want to find the accounts of a customer, we need to perform the following:

1. Look up the customer by their key in the customer table.
2. Join the customer using this key to their accounts.
3. Look up the customer's accounts in the accounts table using the account keys that we found in the previous step.

Contrast this with the left-hand side of the figure, and you will see that the model is much simpler. We find the following elements:

1. A node for the customer.

2. Three nodes for the accounts.

3. Three relationships linking the accounts to the customer.

Finding the accounts of the customer is as simple as performing the following:

1. Finding the customer through an index lookup on the key that we specify in advance

2. Traversing out from this customer node using the *owns* relationship to the accounts that we need

In the preceding example, we are performing only a single join operation over two tables. This operation will become exponentially more expensive in a relational database management system as the number of join operations increases and logarithmically more expensive as the datasets involved in the join operation become larger and larger. Calculating the Cartesian product of two sets (which is what relational databases need to do in order to perform the join) becomes more and more computationally complex as the tables grow larger.

We hope to have given you some initial pointers with regards to graph modeling compared to relational modeling, and we will now proceed to discuss some pitfalls and best practices.

Graph modeling – best practices and pitfalls

In this chapter, we will give an overview of the generic recommendations and best practices for graph database modeling, and we will also provide you with some insight into common pitfalls for you to avoid. It goes without saying that all of these recommendations are generic recommendations and that there may be exceptions to these rules in your specific domains—just like this could be previously, in the case of your relational database design models.

Graph modeling best practices

In the upcoming sections, I will be sharing and discussing a number of practices that have been successfully applied in a number of Neo4j projects.

Design for query-ability

Like with any database management system, but perhaps even more so for a graph database management system such as Neo4j, your queries will drive your model. What we mean with this is that, exactly like it was with any type of database that you may have used in the past or would still be using today, you will need to make specific design decisions based on specific trade-offs. Therefore, it follows that there is no *one perfect way to model* in a graph database such as Neo4j. It will all depend on the questions that you want to ask of the data, and this will drive your design and your model.

Therefore, my number one and undoubtedly the most important best practice for graph database modeling is to start with your user story. What does the user of the system that you are designing want to know from the data? An example of such a story could be something like this:

> *"as an employee, I want to know who in the company I work for has similar skills to me so that we can exchange knowledge"*

This excerpt tells a little bit about the entities that I need to include in the model and the connections that should exist between these entities. Different domain descriptions would probably add similar or different entities and similar or different connections and will then gradually complete your model.

Align relationships with use cases

One of the ways that you can model for `query-ability` and let your queries drive your model is by using the different relationship types that you can have between nodes for different use cases. Many great graph database models use multiple relationships between two of the same nodes for different use case scenarios.

One of the reasons why this recommended best practice is actually applicable and of real use in practical development efforts is that the specialization tax, which is the price that you, as a developer, pay (mostly in terms of added model complexity) for introducing a specific relationship between two nodes for a specific use case — for introducing this additional relationship is in fact so low. There are no additional tables or schemas to be created, and to be even more specific, there are no additional joins to be computed. All that happens is that the graph traversals will use different paths to establish their course across the network stored in the database.

A key concept to be kept in mind when aligning relationships with use cases is the naming strategy for your relationship types. The general recommendation is to use as few generic names such as HAS_A or IS_PART_OF as possible, but to be more specific in these naming efforts.

Look for n-ary relationships

Sometimes, you will find that the first reading of your user stories will not yield optimal results. Obviously, there can be many reasons for this, but this is often because there are some *hidden* model elements in these stories that we did not spot at first.

One of the cases where we often see this is when dealing with the so-called n-ary relationships. These types of relationships are often hidden in the model when we want to associate more than two things; in some cases, the natural and convenient way to represent certain concepts is to use relations to link a concept to more than just one concept. These relations are called n-ary relations because they can serve more than two (in fact, *n*) things or concepts. It is a very common modeling pattern.

When we discover these types of relationships in a graph model, this typically means that there's an additional node to discover that we have split out a new entity.

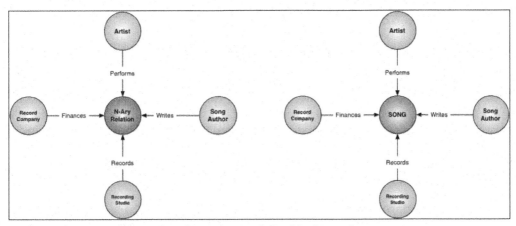

Transforming n-ary relationships into nodes

This is exactly what we have done in the preceding example.

Granulate nodes

The typical graph modeling pattern that we will discuss in this section will be called the granulate pattern. This means that in graph database modeling, we will tend to have much more fine-grained data models with a higher level of "granularity" than we would be used to having in a relational model.

In a relational model, we use a process called database normalization to come up with the granularity of our model. Wikipedia defines this process as:

> *"…the process of organizing the fields and tables of a relational database to minimize redundancy and dependency. Normalization usually involves dividing large tables into smaller (and less redundant) tables and defining relationships between them. The objective is to isolate data so that additions, deletions, and modifications of a field can be made in just one table and then propagated through the rest of the database using the defined relationships."*

The reality of this process is that we will create smaller and smaller table structures until we reach the third normal form. This is a convention that the IT industry seems to have agreed on—a database is considered to have been normalized as soon as it achieves the third normal form. Visit `http://en.wikipedia.org/wiki/Database_normalization#Normal_forms` for more details.

As we discussed before, this model can be quite expensive, as it effectively introduces the need for join tables and join operations at query time. Database administrators tend to denormalize the data for this very reason, which introduces data-duplication—another very tricky problem to manage.

In graph database modeling, however, normalization is much cheaper for the simple reason that these infamous join operations are much easier to perform. This is why we see a clear tendency in graph models to create "thin" nodes and relationships, that is, nodes and relationships with few properties on them. These nodes and relationships are very granular and have been "granulated".

Related to this pattern is a typical question that we get asked and ask ourselves in every modeling session: should I keep this as a property or should the property become its own node? For example, should we model the alcohol percentage of a beer as a property on a beer brand? The following diagram shows the model with the alcohol percentage as a property:

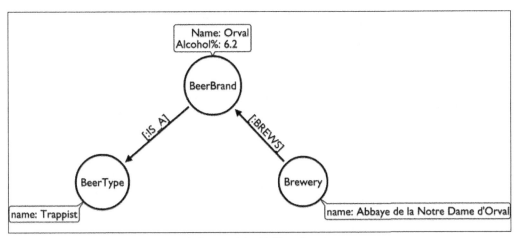

A data model with "fatter" nodes

The alternative would be to split the alcohol percentage off as a different kind of node. The following diagram illustrates this:

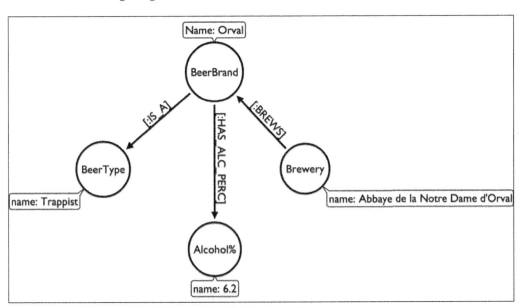

A data model with a "granulated" node structure

Which one of these models is right? I would say both and neither. The real fundamental thing here is that we should be looking at our queries to determine which version is appropriate. In general, I would argue that:

- If we don't need to evaluate the alcohol percentage during the course of a graph traversal, we are probably better off keeping it as a property of the end node of the traversal. After all, we keep our model a bit simpler when doing this, and everyone appreciates simplicity.

- If we need to evaluate the alcohol percentage of a particular (set of) beer brands during the course of our graph traversal, then splitting it off into its own node category is probably a good idea. Traversing through a node is often easier and faster than evaluating properties for each and every path.

As we will see in the next paragraph, many people actually take this approach even a step further by working with in-graph indexes.

Use in-graph indexes when appropriate

Taking the granulate pattern even further and knowing that most indexing technologies actually use graphs/trees under the hood anyway, we can apply this pattern to create natural indexes for our data models, inside the graph. This can be very useful for specific types of query patterns: range queries, time series, proximity searches, and so on.

Looking at our previous little beer model, the alcohol percentages could be a prime candidate for these in-graph indexes. The idea here is that we connect all of the alcohol percentages to one another and create a linked list of alcohol percentages that we could follow upward or downward, for example, to find beer brands with similar alcohol percentages within a certain range. The model is displayed in the following diagram:

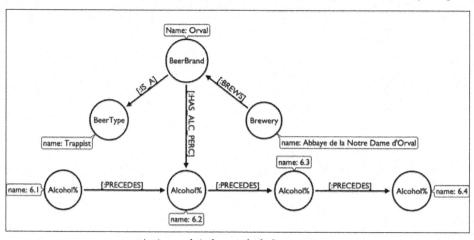

An in-graph index on alcohol percentages

These types of index structures are very often used to deal with time data in a graph structure. In this case, we create more of a time tree instead of a time line and connect our graph data to this tree instead of putting timestamps as properties on every node or relationship. The following diagram contains an example of such a tree structure:

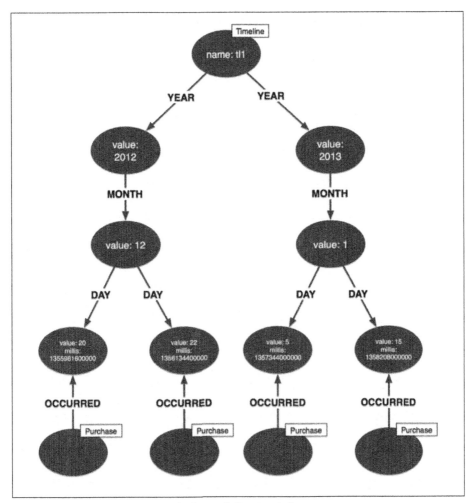

An in-graph time-tree index

All of the patterns in the preceding diagram are common modeling patterns that have been used successfully in projects. Use them wisely, and always remember that it's all about the query patterns. Knowing what the questions you want to ask of the data are will massively impact its design model, and chances are that you will need and want to iterate over that model multiple times to get it to a stable state. Fortunately, graph database management systems such as Neo4j deal with this kind of variation quite elegantly and allow you to do exactly this when appropriate.

Graph database modeling pitfalls

As with any type of database modeling, a graph database will also have some pitfalls that we would want to try and avoid. This section will by no means attempt to give you an exhaustive list, but should give you a feel for the types of practices that can lead to poor modeling decisions.

Using "rich" properties

As it is actually a best practice to have a very granular model in in-graph database systems, the opposite of this can often be an antipattern. Using properties on a node that are ostensibly too rich (as shown in the following figure) can be much better solved by leveraging the model, splitting off the properties into separate nodes, and connecting them using a relationship:

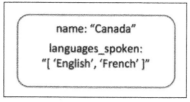

Using "rich" properties

Look at the following diagram for a potential solution to this antipattern:

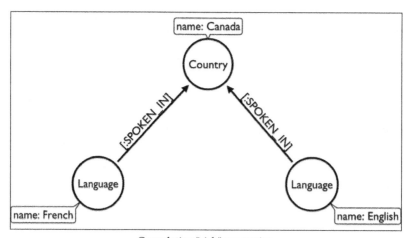

Granulating "rich" properties

Node representing multiple concepts

Another antipattern that we have seen being introduced a number of times is that different concerns or concepts are not separated appropriately in a model. In the model represented in the following figure, we are mingling together the country concept, the language concept, and the currency concept in one node structure:

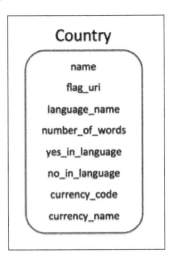

This should be a red flag, as it will inevitably present us with problems or limitations at query time. It will be far wiser to split off the concepts into separate country, language, and currency node structures, each with their own characteristics and properties. This is what we are trying to convey in the following corrected figure (as follows):

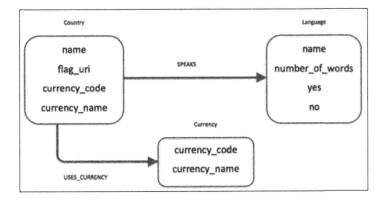

Unconnected graphs

A perhaps obvious example of graph modeling antipatterns are the unconnected graphs. Graphs are all about the connections between entities, and the power of graph databases is all in the traversals of these connections from node to node. A pattern like the one displayed in the following image should really not be used in a graph database:

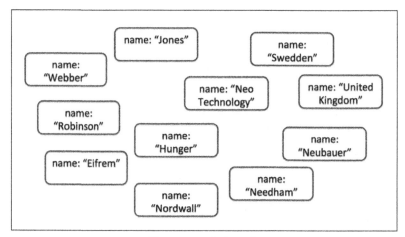

The unconnected graph

Relationships provide structure and query power in a graph, so not using relationships leaves a wealth of opportunities underutilized.

The dense node pattern

We discussed before how graph queries work in a graph database system. The basic principle was that of a graph local query: starting at a (set of) well-defined starting point(s) and then crawling out from there. The traversal speed is typically very fast and only dependent on the number of parts of the graph that the query will touch or traverse through. Typically, traversal speeds are also very constant with growing dataset sizes, simply because in a normal graph model, *everything is not connected to everything*. The query will only evaluate the parts of the graph that are connected to the starting points, and therefore, the traversal speeds will be flat.

A very interesting problem then occurs in datasets where some parts of the graph are all connected to the same node. This node, also referred to as a dense node or a supernode, becomes a real problem for graph traversals because the graph database management system will have to evaluate all of the connected relationships to that node in order to determine what the next step will be in the graph traversal. Supernodes can be a real issue in graph database models and should be avoided when setting up your Neo4j instances.

Different strategies exist to deal with this density problem, and Neo Technology is making some important changes to Neo4j to make this problem easier to deal with, but the fact of the matter is that on most occasions we will want to avoid hitting this technical risk by adapting our model. The following diagram highlights one potential strategy that you can use from the music artist/fan graph domain:

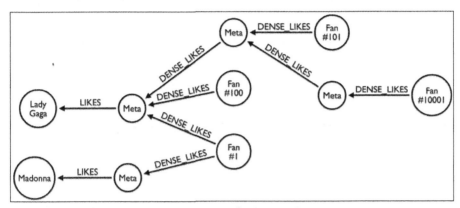

Fan-out strategy for dense nodes

As you can see from the preceding diagram, the strategy essentially consists of "fanning out" the dense relationships to **Lady Gaga** and **Madonna**. Instead of having direct connections from millions of fans to these two popular artists, we create a fan-like structure that connects fans to metanodes, interconnects the metanodes, and then finally connects the top of the metanode hierarchy to the actual artist. The recommendation then becomes that every metanode should have approximately 100 DENSE_LIKES relationships to connect fans to artists and that you can very quickly traverse these relationships to figure out whether there is a variable-length path to connect fans to artists.

Other strategies exist for this, and as we mentioned before, the problem is likely to be significantly reduced in future versions of Neo4j, but just from a modeling perspective, it is very useful to be aware and conscious of this pattern and deal with it proactively.

Test questions

Q1. The four fundamental data constructs of Neo4j are:

1. Table, record, field, and constraint
2. Node, relationship, property, and schema
3. Node, relationship, property, and label
4. Document, relationship, property, and collection

Q2. Normalization is expensive in a graph database model.

1. True
2. False

Q3. If you have a few entities in your dataset that have lots of relationships to other entities, then you can't use a graph database because of the dense node problem.

1. True—you will have to use a relational system
2. True—but there is no alternative, so you will have to live with it
3. False—you can still use a graph database but it will be painfully slow for all queries
4. False—you can very effectively use a graph database, but you should take precautions, for example, applying a fan-out pattern to your data

Summary

In this chapter, we discussed a number of topics that will help you get started when modeling your domain for a graph database management system. We talked about the fundamental building blocks of the model, compared and contrasted this with the way we do things in a relational database management system, and then discussed some often recurring patterns, both good and bad, for doing the modeling work.

With the model behind us, we can now start tackling specific business problems using Neo4j. In the next chapter, we will start discussing the different data import strategies that will fill the Neo4j database with domain-specific datasets.

5
Importing Data into Neo4j

Database management systems are meaningless tools without their data. It really goes without saying. So how do we get data into a graph database management system like Neo4j? There really is no one specific answer, and in this chapter, we will try to give you a couple of pointers towards potential solutions.

It is important to point out that this has a very immediate and direct link to the previous chapter. After all, importing data without a model is pointless—it would never serve a real-world purpose, as it would never be able to answer the data queries of the user. As we previously indicated, but it does not hurt pointing it out again, graph models are tremendously important, and you need to think these through before you consider importing the data. We will, however, assume that you have taken this advice to heart and get on with the question of how to import data into Neo4j.

We will cover the following topics:

- Alternative approaches to importing data in Neo4j
- Available tooling options to help us import the data
- Example scenarios to illustrate specific ways to successfully import your dataset

Let's get started.

Alternative approaches to importing data into Neo4j

The first thing everyone should understand is that in a connected world, importing data is, per definition, more difficult to do. It is a true *knot* that is terribly difficult to untie for many different reasons, but that does not mean that we cannot untie it!

Logically, the problem of importing *connected* data is technically more difficult than with *unconnected* data structures. Importing unconnected data (for example, the nodes of your graph model) is always easy/easier. Just dump it all in there. However, you then come to importing the connections and relationships, and you find that there's no such thing as an **external entity** (also known as **the database schema**) that will ensure the consistency and connectedness of the import. You have to do this yourself, and explicitly by importing the relationships between the following:

- A start node that you have to find
- An end node that you have to look up

This process is just inherently more complicated than what it would be in other data models, especially at scale.

So how do we untie this knot? We can really see two steps that everyone needs to take in order to do so:

- **Understand the import problem**: Every import is different, just like every graph is different. There is little or no uniformity there, and in spite of the fact that many people would love to just have a silver bullet solution to this problem, the fact of the matter is that there is none. Therefore, we will have to *create* a more or less complex import solution for every use case using one of the tools at hand. However, like with any problem, understanding the import problem is often the key to choosing the right solution, and this is what we will focus on here as well.

- **Pick the right tool**: There are many tools out there, and we should not be defeated by the "law of the instrument" and use the right tool for the job. Therefore, in this chapter, we will first try to bring these different tools together, bring some structure to them, and then provide some examples. This should allow you to make some kind of mapping between the different types of import problems and the different tools at hand.

Let's start by looking at the different types of import scenarios and the tools that you have at your disposal.

Know your import problem – choose your tooling

Choosing the right import solution for your use case starts with properly understanding what kind of import scenario you have before you. The following mind map should allow you to better understand the scenario:

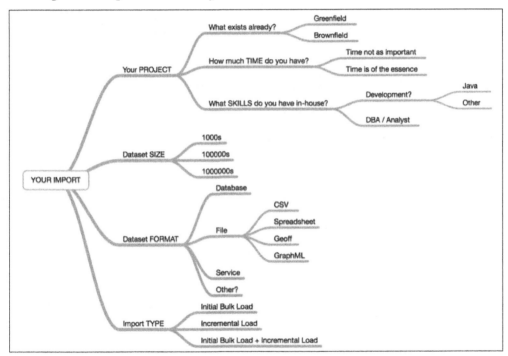

Your import use case

In my experience, most scenarios fit in here somewhere. If yours does not, then please contact me. We can now try to understand what the options would be in terms of technical import tools:

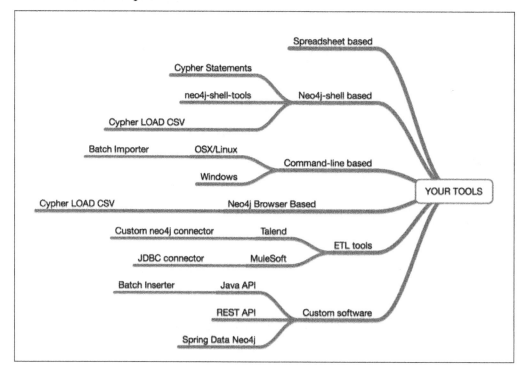

It would lead us too far to try to match all the different scenarios to all the different toolsets, but perhaps we can make some useful assessments of the pros and cons of the different tools, as follows:

Tools	Pros	Cons
Spreadsheets	It is very easy to use. All you need to do is write some formulas that concatenate strings with cell content and compose cypher statements this way. These cypher statements can then just be copied into the Neo4j-shell.	• Only works at a limited scale (< 5000 nodes/ relationships at a time) • Performance is not good — overhead of unparameterized cypher transactions • Quirks in copying/pasting the statements above a certain scale • Piping the statements can work on OS X/Linux but not on Windows
Neo4j-shell		
Cypher Statements	Native toolset — no need to install anything else. Neo4j-shell can be used to pipe in OS X/Linux, which can be very handy.	You have to create the statements (see above). If they are not parameterized, they will be slow because of the parsing overhead.
Neo4j-shell-tools	A fantastic, rich functionality for importing CSV, GEOFF, and GraphML files.	Not a part of the product (yet). Requires a separate installation.
Cypher Load CSV	A rich functionality to import CSV files straight from cypher.	New toolset — recently released and under rapid development.
Neo4j Browser		
Cypher Load CSV	A rich functionality to import CSV files straight from cypher.	New toolset — still under development at the time of writing.
Command line		
batch importer	High performance, easy to use, especially with binary installer.	Specific purpose for CSV files.

Tools	Pros	Cons
ETL tools		
Talend	Out of the box, versatile, customizable, uses specific Neo4j connector both in online and offline modes.	Requires you to learn Talend. The current connector is not yet upgraded to Neo4j 2.0.
MuleSoft	Out of the box, versatile, customizable, uses the JDBC connector in the online mode.	Requires you to learn MuleSoft. Batch loading of offline databases is not supported.
Custom software		
Java API	High performance, perfectly customizable, supports different input types specific for your use case!	You have to write the code!
REST API		
Spring Data Neo4j		

With this overview with us, we will now spend the rest of this chapter explaining how you can use some of the most commonly used import techniques to get you going with Neo4j.

Importing small(ish) datasets

In this section, we will give you a few examples of how you can import small(ish) datasets into Neo4j. Small-ish means comfortably importing anything from a few hundred nodes to a few hundred thousand nodes and relationships and importing larger datasets with considerable patience.

We will present three approaches in this section:

- Importing using spreadsheets
- Importing using Neo4j-shell-tools
- Importing using Load CSV

All of these approaches have specific pros and cons, and it depends on your specific situation to choose your most appropriate option.

Importing data using spreadsheets

Many people work with spreadsheets and are comfortable manipulating their data in this environment. This is why for smaller datasets, this is often a very suitable way of importing your data. The process is very simple:

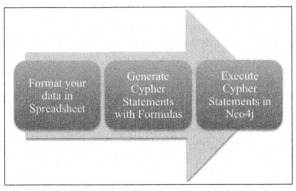

Spreadsheet import process

This approach works in most of the common spreadsheet solutions out there (Microsoft Excel, Open Office Calc, Google Sheets, Apple Numbers) as it relies on a very simple mechanism: using string concatenation based on cell values to compose a query statement. Let's take a brief look at this.

First, let's assume that we have a simple data table with *people* like the one in the following figure. These people have a unique identifier (first column), a name (second column), and a type/label (third column):

	B	C	D
2	Node	Name	Label
3	1	Amada Emory	Female
4	2	Rana Seely	Female
5	3	Detra Thatcher	Female
6	4	Melda Reza	Female
7	5	Shana Willems	Female
8	6	Sharonda Peele	Female
9	7	Dagny Agee	Female
10	8	Tisa Woodman	Female
11	9	Shelba Mutchler	Female
12	10	Anderson Spagnola	Male
13	11	Pamala Forward	Female
14	12	Melva Fairchild	Female
15	13	Antione Selman	Male
16	14	Carmelia Cali	Female
17	15	Fairy Daughtery	Female
18	16	Stefany Mcamis	Female
19	17	Kermit Meaney	Male
20	18	Williemae Dossantos	Female
21	19	Marth Sparling	Female
22	20	Jarvis Noland	Male

Nodes in a spreadsheet

Let's also assume that in order to import this data in a meaningful way into a graph database management system like Neo4j, we would have some additional information about the relationships between these people:

	H	I	J	K	L
2	From	Name	Relationship Type	To	Name
3	1	Amada Emory	MOTHER_OF	11	Pamala Forward
4	1	Amada Emory	MOTHER_OF	12	Melva Fairchild
5	1	Amada Emory	MOTHER_OF	13	Antione Selman
6	2	Rana Seely	MOTHER_OF	14	Carmelia Cali
7	2	Rana Seely	MOTHER_OF	15	Fairy Daughtery
8	2	Rana Seely	MOTHER_OF	16	Stefany Mcamis
9	3	Detra Thatcher	MOTHER_OF	17	Kermit Meaney
10	3	Detra Thatcher	MOTHER_OF	18	Williemae Dossantos
11	3	Detra Thatcher	MOTHER_OF	19	Marth Sparling
12	10	Anderson Spagnola	FATHER_OF	20	Jarvis Noland
13	14	Carmelia Cali	MOTHER_OF	1	Amada Emory
14	11	Pamala Forward	MOTHER_OF	2	Rana Seely
15	11	Pamala Forward	MOTHER_OF	3	Detra Thatcher
16	12	Melva Fairchild	MOTHER_OF	4	Melda Reza
17	12	Melva Fairchild	MOTHER_OF	5	Shana Willems
18	12	Melva Fairchild	MOTHER_OF	6	Sharonda Peele
19	17	Kermit Meaney	FATHER_OF	7	Dagny Agee
20	13	Antione Selman	MOTHER_OF	8	Tisa Woodman
21	13	Antione Selman	MOTHER_OF	9	Shelba Mutchler
22	20	Jarvis Noland	FATHER_OF	1	Amada Emory

Relationships in a spreadsheet

Using the string concatenation function of your favorite spreadsheet program, you can then create two formulas that will look something like these:

- One formula to create the nodes of your graph:

$$f_x \quad | = \text{"create}(\text{n:"}\&D3\&\text{"}\{\text{id:"}\&B3\&\text{", name:'"}\&C3\&\text{"'}\});\text{"}$$

- One formula to create the relationships of your graph:

$$f_x \quad | = \text{"match}(\text{from}\{\text{id:"}\&H3\&\text{"}\}),(\text{to}\{\text{id:"}\&K3\&\text{"}\})\text{create from-}[\text{:"}\&J3\&\text{"}]\text{->to;"}$$

So, using this approach, you can create a long list of cypher statements that will allow you to create your graph by simply executing them.

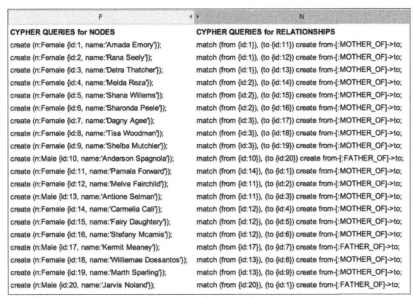

CYPHER QUERIES for NODES	CYPHER QUERIES for RELATIONSHIPS
create (n:Female {id:1, name:'Amada Emory'});	match (from {id:1}), (to {id:11}) create from-[:MOTHER_OF]->to;
create (n:Female {id:2, name:'Rana Seely'});	match (from {id:1}), (to {id:12}) create from-[:MOTHER_OF]->to;
create (n:Female {id:3, name:'Detra Thatcher'});	match (from {id:1}), (to {id:13}) create from-[:MOTHER_OF]->to;
create (n:Female {id:4, name:'Melda Reza'});	match (from {id:2}), (to {id:14}) create from-[:MOTHER_OF]->to;
create (n:Female {id:5, name:'Shana Willems'});	match (from {id:2}), (to {id:15}) create from-[:MOTHER_OF]->to;
create (n:Female {id:6, name:'Sharonda Peele'});	match (from {id:2}), (to {id:16}) create from-[:MOTHER_OF]->to;
create (n:Female {id:7, name:'Dagny Agee'});	match (from {id:3}), (to {id:17}) create from-[:MOTHER_OF]->to;
create (n:Female {id:8, name:'Tisa Woodman'});	match (from {id:3}), (to {id:18}) create from-[:MOTHER_OF]->to;
create (n:Female {id:9, name:'Shelba Mutchler'});	match (from {id:3}), (to {id:19}) create from-[:MOTHER_OF]->to;
create (n:Male {id:10, name:'Anderson Spagnola'});	match (from {id:10}), (to {id:20}) create from-[:FATHER_OF]->to;
create (n:Female {id:11, name:'Pamala Forward'});	match (from {id:14}), (to {id:1}) create from-[:MOTHER_OF]->to;
create (n:Female {id:12, name:'Melva Fairchild'});	match (from {id:11}), (to {id:2}) create from-[:MOTHER_OF]->to;
create (n:Male {id:13, name:'Antione Selman'});	match (from {id:11}), (to {id:3}) create from-[:MOTHER_OF]->to;
create (n:Female {id:14, name:'Carmelia Cali'});	match (from {id:12}), (to {id:4}) create from-[:MOTHER_OF]->to;
create (n:Female {id:15, name:'Fairy Daughtery'});	match (from {id:12}), (to {id:5}) create from-[:MOTHER_OF]->to;
create (n:Female {id:16, name:'Stefany Mcamis'});	match (from {id:12}), (to {id:6}) create from-[:MOTHER_OF]->to;
create (n:Male {id:17, name:'Kermit Meaney'});	match (from {id:17}), (to {id:7}) create from-[:FATHER_OF]->to;
create (n:Female {id:18, name:'Williemae Dossantos'});	match (from {id:13}), (to {id:8}) create from-[:MOTHER_OF]->to;
create (n:Female {id:19, name:'Marth Sparling'});	match (from {id:13}), (to {id:9}) create from-[:MOTHER_OF]->to;
create (n:Male {id:20, name:'Jarvis Noland'});	match (from {id:20}), (to {id:1}) create from-[:FATHER_OF]->to;

Cypher queries in a spreadsheet

Executing these queries can be as simple as copying and pasting them into the Neo4j browser or shell, or (and this is probably the better option) putting them into a text file and either piping it into the shell (using the | operator on Unix-based systems) or uploading it to the Neo4j server. The Neo4j browser has a specific functionality to drop a file onto the browser web application and execute the queries:

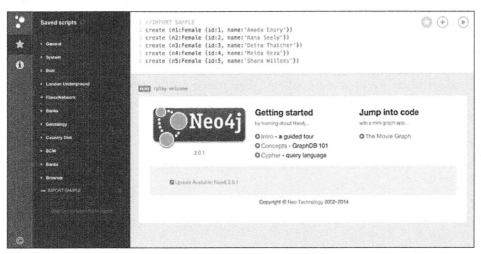

Running the spreadsheet queries

The end result will then be our graph database with the imported data, which we can interactively query from the browser:

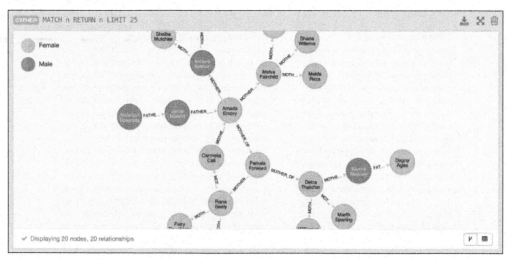

The resulting database from the spreadsheet

As mentioned before, this system works very well for smaller imports, but we will want to use different mechanisms for somewhat larger imports. Let's start exploring these.

Importing using Neo4j-shell-tools

As you probably know by now, the Neo4j system also has a command-line utility that you can access by executing the following command from the terminal in your main Neo4j directory (or `bin\neo4shell.bat` on Windows machines):

```
bin/Neo4j-shell
```

In this shell, you can not only execute cypher commands, but you can also extend the shell with some additional tools. At the time of writing this book, installing these tools is very easy: just download and extract them in Neo4j's `lib` directory. Here's how you can do this:

```
cd /path/to/your/Neo4j/server
curl http://dist.Neo4j.org/jexp/shell/Neo4j-shell-tools-2.0.zip -o Neo4j-shell-tools.zip
unzip Neo4j-shell-tools.zip -d lib
```

Once you have done this, the shell should be equipped with a new import functionality. This functionality works as follows:

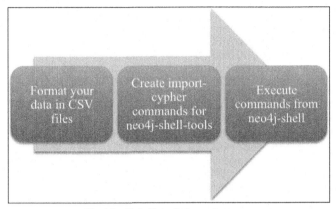

The Neo4j-shell-tools import process

Let's try this for the same dataset as in the previously used spreadsheet example. We will create two .csv files in this case: one for nodes (nodes.csv) and one for relationships (rels.csv). Here's the nodes.csv file for you to take a look at:

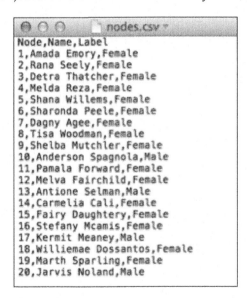

Here's the `rels.csv` file that we will be using:

```
●○○                    rels.csv
From,Name,Relationship Type,To,Name
1,Amada Emory,MOTHER_OF,11,Pamala Forward
1,Amada Emory,MOTHER_OF,12,Melva Fairchild
1,Amada Emory,MOTHER_OF,13,Antione Selman
2,Rana Seely,MOTHER_OF,14,Carmelia Cali
2,Rana Seely,MOTHER_OF,15,Fairy Daughtery
2,Rana Seely,MOTHER_OF,16,Stefany Mcamis
3,Detra Thatcher,MOTHER_OF,17,Kermit Meaney
3,Detra Thatcher,MOTHER_OF,18,Williemae Dossantos
3,Detra Thatcher,MOTHER_OF,19,Marth Sparling
10,Anderson Spagnola,FATHER_OF,20,Jarvis Noland
14,Carmelia Cali,MOTHER_OF,1,Amada Emory
11,Pamala Forward,MOTHER_OF,2,Rana Seely
11,Pamala Forward,MOTHER_OF,3,Detra Thatcher
12,Melva Fairchild,MOTHER_OF,4,Melda Reza
12,Melva Fairchild,MOTHER_OF,5,Shana Willems
12,Melva Fairchild,MOTHER_OF,6,Sharonda Peele
17,Kermit Meaney,FATHER_OF,7,Dagny Agee
13,Antione Selman,MOTHER_OF,8,Tisa Woodman
13,Antione Selman,MOTHER_OF,9,Shelba Mutchler
20,Jarvis Noland,FATHER_OF,1,Amada Emory
```

Then, using the Neo4j-shell-tools syntax, we want to execute two commands to populate our database. We can prepare these in our favorite text editor as follows:

```
●○○            import-shell-tools.txt — Edited
// create nodes
import-cypher -d , -i ./IMPORT/INPUT/nodes.csv -o ./IMPORT/OUTPUT/
nodesoutput.txt create (n:#{Label} {id:{Node},name:{Name}}) return *

//create rels
import-cypher -d , -i ./IMPORT/INPUT/rels.csv -o ./IMPORT/OUTPUT/
relsoutput.txt MATCH (from {id:{From}}), (to {id:{To}}) create from-
[:#{Relationship Type}]->to return *
```

Neo4j-shell-tools commands

Executing the following query in the shell gives us immediate results:

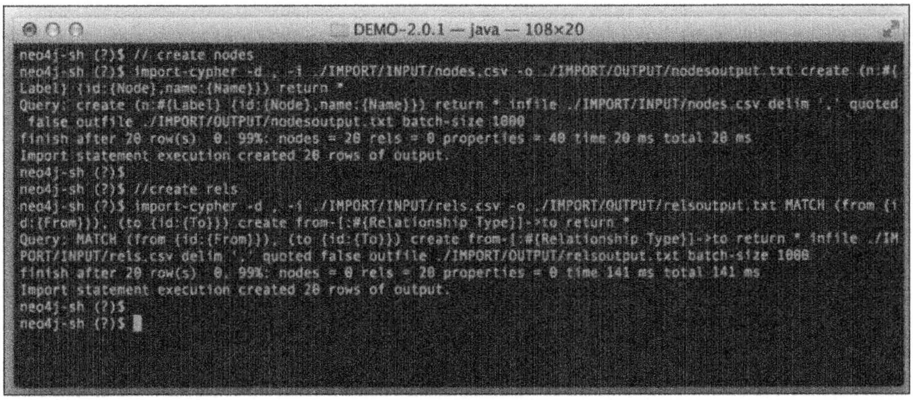

Neo4j-shell-tools result

The generated graph will then immediately be accessible in the Neo4j browser. The result, of course, will be identical to the graph shown previously

The Neo4j-shell-tools are much more powerful than what we have highlighted in these few paragraphs. It allows for different delimiters, quoted values, and variable batch sizes to tweak the performance of the import. It also supports other file formats such as the **GEOFF** and **GraphML** formats and supports exporting to many of these formats as well. So all in all, it is a very potential tool that can probably scale for importing millions of nodes and relationships—but not for billions. We will address this use case a bit later.

Now, we will finish this section by treating a very new methodology—Load CSV.

Importing using Load CSV

During the course of 2013, Neo Technology saw a very steep ramp in adoption for Neo4j and started getting a lot more user feedback. One of the most prominent pieces of consistent feedback was that Neo4j needed to improve its native import capabilities, and this is why this feature was added as a capability as part of the 2.1 release of Neo4j.

The import workflow is similar to that of Neo4j-shell-tools, but has the following exceptions:

- It is embedded into cypher.
- The .csv files can be loaded from anywhere; it just needs a URI.

- It is accessible from the new Neo4j browser tool.
- It does not yet (at the time of writing this book) allow for variable labels and relationship types. This is somewhat important for us in this example, as it will mean that we cannot immediately assign the right labels and relationship types from the current CSV files; we will have to add these as properties first and then run another cypher query to fix this.

So, let's go through the import of the same files using this final toolset:

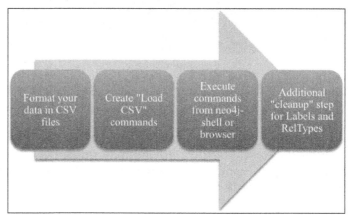

The Load CSV process

Let's start by importing the nodes. Executing the following query in the Neo4j browser works out very well:

```
//Loading CSV with Nodes
load csv with headers from
"file:/your/path/to/nodes.csv"
as nodes
create (n {id: nodes.Node, name: nodes.Name, type: nodes.Label})
return n
```

Executing this query in the Neo4j browser tool gives us the following result:

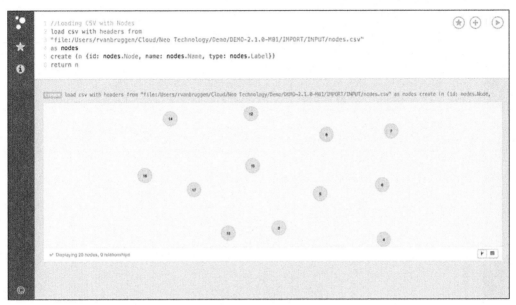

Loading nodes with Load CSV

Then, we will add the relationships to the graph using the following query:

```
//Loading CSV with Rels
load csv with headers from
"file:/your/path/to/rels.csv"
as rels
match (from {id: rels.From}), (to {id: rels.To})
create from-[:REL {type: rels.`Relationship Type`}]->to
return from, to
```

Then, we get the following result that is very similar to what we had in the previous import scenarios:

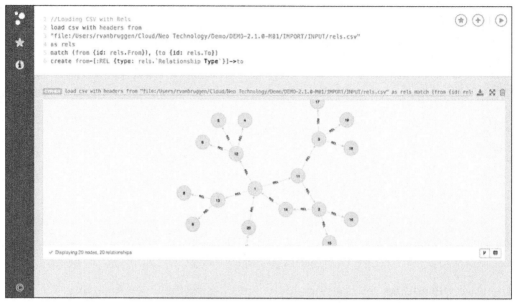

Loading relationships with Load CSV

However, the difference between the current graph and the ones that we had in our previous import scenarios is that we have not used any labels or relationship types yet. Therefore, the preceding screenshot looks a bit different. The following two queries correct this though:

- Query 1:

```
//Assign labels for Males and Females
match (m {type:"Male"}), (f {type:"Female"})
set m:Male, f:Female
return m,f
```

- Query 2:

```
//Create duplicate relationship with appropriate type
match (n)-[r1 {type:"MOTHER_OF"}]->(m), (s)-[r2 {type:"FATHER_
OF"}]->(t)
create n-[:MOTHER_OF]->m, s-[:FATHER_OF]->t
return *;
//Remove duplicate relationships
match ()-[r:REL]-() delete r;
```

The following screenshot shows the final result of Load CSV:

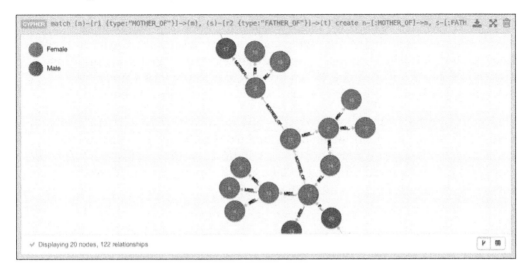

From working with the Load CSV toolset at this early milestone release, it seems clear that there are still quite a few things to iron out, but in general, we still recommend that you take a look at it as it presents you with a very intuitive and native way of importing data into Neo4j. Neo Technology also claims that this approach should work well for imports into millions (but not billions) of nodes and relationships, especially if you want to make use of the periodic commit functionality that is tied to Load CSV. If you start your Load CSV statements with a "using periodic commit {a number}", Neo4j will periodically commit your import transactions, thereby making it a lot easier to scale your import.

For a larger import use case, we will now take a look at a final data import toolset.

Scaling the import

Many users of Neo4j need to import larger datasets into Neo4j, at least for their initial startup use cases. Doing so can be difficult using any of the previous techniques and takes a long time. Although there are a number of things that you can tweak (for example, the batch sizes in Neo4j-shell-tools), there is a limit to the transactional write performance that you will get from running the Neo4j server. This limit is mostly I/O driven because of the transactional qualities of the Neo4j database management system; it basically needs to go down to disk at every commit and can take some time.

This is why Neo Technology and its community have developed an alternative way of creating Neo4j data stores without having the Neo4j server running. This allows the import process to be executed in an *all or nothing* fashion, without doing intermediate commits on the underlying component transactions. The import will either succeed or fail in its entirety. This nontransactional approach to importing is much faster—literally bringing down imports that would take hours in a transactional fashion to minutes or even seconds in a nontransactional import.

The batch importer, as this tool is called, is not bundled with Neo4j. At the time of writing this book, you can download this tool from `https://github.com/jexp/batch-import/tree/20` and follow the installation instructions to get it active on your system. Once you do this, we can take a look at how this batch import process works with the help of the following diagram:

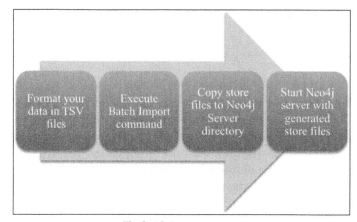

The batch import process

As with the previous import scenarios, we will start with the same CSV files. However, in order for these to fit the more specific format of the batch importer, we have to make a few changes:

- The columns of the files have to be tab separated, not comma separated. A find/replace operation is required due to the change in the file structure from the original format that we used in the previous scenarios to this one.

- The relationship file has a specific format that you need to respect, including a specific way of referencing the nodes that are used in building the relationships. Essentially, it boils down to using the row number of the nodes file as start/end identifiers, knowing that the first data row (which is the second row of the file) is referred to as the 0 row. So, there is a bit of data modification that we have to do on our file to make this work, as you can see from the following screenshot. Here's the new `nodes.csv` file:

The TSV file for batch import of nodes

Here is the new `rels.csv` file:

The TSV file for batch import of relationships

Having formatted the files, all we have to do is place them into the batch importer directory and execute a simple command:

```
./import.sh test.db nodes.csv rels.csv
```

In a matter of milliseconds, this small dataset is created:

The result of the batch import process

As explained previously, the output of the batch importer is not what we will immediately see on our Neo4j server. In fact, the output is just a `test.db` directory. This is a set of files that we can then copy to the `/path/to/your/Neo4j/server/data` directory, replacing the `graph.db` directory that you may find in there already. After restarting the Neo4j server, you will then see the dataset that we just imported, and it should look very familiar to the datasets that we imported in the previous scenarios.

Questions and answers

Q1. Neo4j comes with a single, universal data import toolset that will allow you to import any of your datasets, small or large.

1. True
2. False

Answer: False. Importing data into a graph database will require you to think about your import use case and then choose the right tool for the job. Luckily, Neo4j comes with a number of different options that you can choose from.

Q2. Which data formats can you import into Neo4j?

1. Spreadsheets
2. CSV or TSV files
3. GEOFF or GraphML files
4. All of the above

Answer: All of the above. Different tools will allow you to import different formats more or less easily, but all are possible without a doubt.

Q3. The Neo4j batch importer is much faster than any of the other import technologies presented because:

1. It was written in C++ instead of Java
2. It does not write to a running transactional instance of Neo4j and can therefore run un-transactionally
3. It has fewer bugs, which allows it to run faster
4. It uses fancy caching technologies to make it write faster

Answer: It does not write to a running Neo4j instance; all it does is write the store files of the Neo4j server that you can use afterwards on your server.

Summary

This concludes our overview of different data import technologies for the Neo4j database management system. We have presented you with an approach to choose the right import technologies, and then, in some detail, we have explored how at least some of these technologies can be used on a real dataset. There are, of course, other import techniques that we did not discuss. More specifically, a programmatic import using custom software could be useful for you. You should visit some of the Neo4j blogs such as `http://maxdemarzi.com` or `http://jexp.de/blog/` if you are interested in this.

This chapter should give you enough confidence to now start working with your own data domain in the context of Neo4j.

In the next few chapters, we will start applying what we have learned by looking at different use case scenarios that Neo4j is frequently used for and discussing them in some detail.

6
Use Case Example – Recommendations

In this chapter, we will start to look at how we can use the Neo4j graph database for a very specific use case. All the discussions so far have led us to this discussion, where we really want to zoom in on how one would practically use a database such as Neo4j for a very specific use case. We will look at the following topics:

- Modeling product relationships as a graph
- Using relationships to suggest recommendations
- Using relationships to detect fraud

Recommender systems dissected

We will take a look at so-called recommender systems in this chapter. Such systems, broadly speaking, consist of two elementary parts:

- A pattern discovery system: This is the system that somehow figures out what would be a useful recommendation for a particular target group. This discovery can be done in many different ways, but in general we see three ways to do so:

° A business expert who thoroughly understands the domain of the graph database application will use this understanding to determine useful recommendations. For example, the supervisor of a "do-it-yourself" retail outlet would understand a particular pattern. Suppose that if someone came in to buy multiple pots of paint, they would probably also benefit from getting a gentle recommendation for a promotion of high-end brushes. The store has that promotion going on right then, so the recommendation would be very timely. This process would be a discovery process where the pattern that the business expert has discovered would be applied and used in graph databases in real time as part of a sophisticated recommendation.

° A visual discovery of a specific pattern in the graph representation of the business domain. We have found that in many different projects, business users have stumbled upon these kinds of patterns while using graph visualizations to look at their data. Specific patterns emerge, unexpected relations jump out, or, in more advanced visualization solutions, specific clusters of activity all of a sudden become visible and require further investigation. Graph databases such as Neo4j, and the visualization solutions that complement it, can play a wonderfully powerful role in this process.

° An algorithmic discovery of a pattern in a dataset of the business domain using machine learning algorithms to uncover previously unknown patterns in the data. Typically, these processes require an iterative, raw number-crunching approach that has also been used on non-graph data formats in the past. It remains part-art part-science at this point, but can of course yield interesting insights if applied correctly.

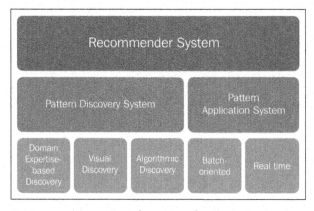

An overview of recommender systems

- **A pattern application system**: All recommender systems will be more or less successful based on not just the patterns that they are able to discover, but also based on the way that they are able to apply these patterns in business applications. We can look at different types of applications for these patterns:

    ○ **Batch-oriented applications**: Some applications of these patterns are not as time-critical as one would expect. It does not really matter in any material kind of way if a bulk e-mail with recommendations, or worse, a printed voucher with recommended discounted products, gets delivered to the customer or prospect at 10 am or 11 am. Batch solutions can usually cope with these kinds of requests, even if they do so in the most inefficient way.

    ○ **Real-time oriented applications**: Some pattern applications simply have to be delivered in real time, in between a web request and a web response, and cannot be precalculated. For these types of systems, which typically use more complex database queries in order to match for the appropriate recommendation to make, graph databases such as Neo4j are a fantastic tool to have. We will illustrate this going forward.

With this classification behind us, we will look at an example dataset and some example queries to make this topic come alive.

Using a graph model for recommendations

We will be using a very specific data model for our recommender system, which is based on the dataset that we imported in the previous chapter. All we have changed is that we added a couple of products and brands to the model, and inserted some data into the database correspondingly. In total, we added the following:

- Ten products
- Three product brands
- Fifty relationships between existing person nodes and the mentioned products, highlighting that these persons *bought* these products

These are the products and brands that we added:

Node	Name	Label
100	iPad	Product
101	iPhone	Product
102	iPad Mini	Product
103	MacBook Pro	Product
104	MacBook Air	Product
105	ChromeBook	Product
106	Samsung Galaxy 4	Product
107	Samsung Galaxy Tab 3	Product
108	Google Nexus 5	Product
109	Google Nexus 7	Product
200	Apple	Brand
201	Google	Brand
202	Samsung	Brand

Adding products and brands to the dataset

The following diagram shows the resulting model:

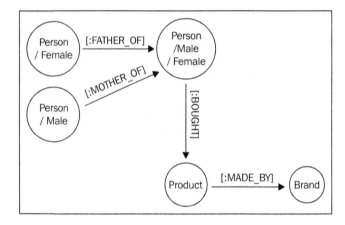

In Neo4j, that model will look something like the following:

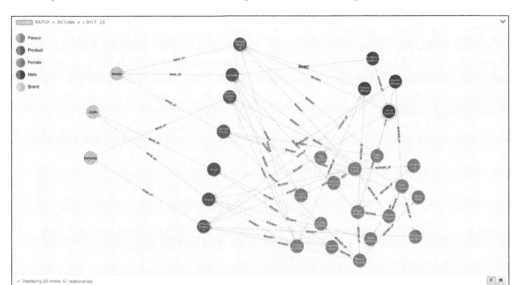

A graph model for our recommender model

A dataset like this one, while of course a broad simplification, offers us some interesting possibilities for a recommender system. Let's take a look at some queries that could really match this use case, and that would allow us to either visually or in real time exploit the data in this dataset in a product recommendation application.

Specific query examples for recommendations

In this example dataset, we are going to explore a couple of interesting queries that would allow us — with the information that is available to us — to construct interesting recommendations for our hypothetical users. We will do so along different *axes*:

- Product purchases
- Brand loyalty
- Social and/or family ties

Let's start with the first and work our way through.

Recommendations based on product purchases

Let's build this thing from the ground up. The first query we want to write is based on past purchasing behavior. We would like to find people that already share a couple of products that they have purchased in the past, but that also explicitly do not share a number of other products. In our data model, this Cypher query would go something like this:

```
match (p1:Person)-[:BOUGHT]->(prod1:Product)<-[:BOUGHT]-(p2:Person)-
[:BOUGHT]->(prod2:Product)
where not(p1-[:BOUGHT]->prod2)
return p1.name as FirstPerson, p2.name as SecondPerson, prod1.name as
CommonProduct, prod2.name as RecommendedProduct;
```

In this query, the `match` clause gathers the pattern of users (p1 and p2) that have bought a common product (prod1), but ensures that p2 has actually bought one or more product(s) that p1 has not bought.

The result is actually quite an extensive list of recommendations, as shown in the following screenshot:

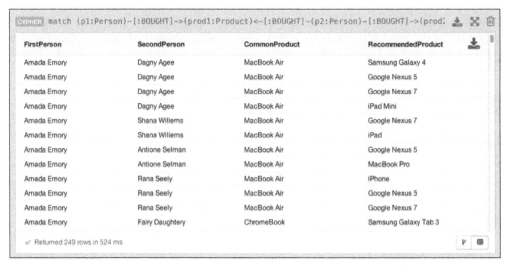

So we can probably do with some refining there.

The next step in our recommendation process would therefore be to look at two people that have a stronger similarity. This means that the two people would need to have bought more than two products in common before the recommended product would actually be assumed to be attractive to the target audience.

Let's look at this query:

```
match (p1:Person)-[:BOUGHT]->(prod1:Product)<-[:BOUGHT]-(p2:Person)-
[:BOUGHT]->(prod2:Product)
with p1,p2,count(prod1) as NrOfSharedProducts, collect(prod1) as
SharedProducts,prod2
where not(p1-[:BOUGHT]->prod2) AND NrOfSharedProducts > 2
return p1.name as FirstPerson, p2.name as SecondPerson, extract(x
in SharedProducts | x.name) as SharedProducts, prod2.name as
RecommendedProduct;
```

As you can see, the basic query is the same as the previous one but we have added some filters for the number of shared products. We also worked with the collection of products (`collect(prod1)`) and extracted the names of these products in the final result. It looks like what is shown in the following screenshot:

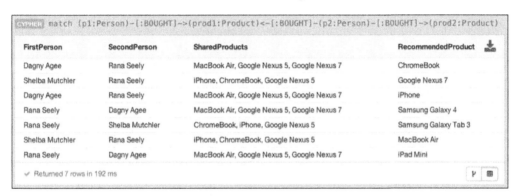

The refined recommendations based on product purchases

So let's now take a look at another type of recommendation, based on brand loyalty.

Recommendations based on brand loyalty

Obviously, we all understand that if we already own a product of a particular brand, it is likely that we will be more interested in other products that are manufactured by that same brand. So let's find the people that already have more than one product of a certain brand and see if we can recommend other products by that brand. Here's the query example:

```
match (p:Person)-[b:BOUGHT]->(prod1:Product)-[:MADE_BY]->(br:Brand)<-
[MADE_BY]-(prod2:Product)
with p, br, prod2, count(prod1) as NrOfBrandProducts
where not(p-[:BOUGHT]->prod2) and NrOfBrandProducts > 1
return p.name as Person, br.name as Brand, collect(prod2.name) as
RecommendedProducts
order by Person ASC;
```

The pattern should be fairly similar, but the difference is that we are now counting the number of products of a certain brand and ensuring that the person in question has not yet bought the other products of that same brand. The result looks like this:

The recommendations based on brand

Again, this gives us some useful recommendations, based on a very different qualifier. Let's then bring in another parameter: our social relationships, in this case, based on the family ties that a particular user will have.

Recommendations based on social ties

In the next version of our recommendation queries, we will be using the relationships—in this particular dataset, based on family ties between parents and/or siblings—between our users to come up with some useful recommendations for their next purchase.

Let's look at the following query:

```
match (p:Person)-[b:BOUGHT]->(prod:Product),p<-[r1]-(parent:Person)-
[r2]->(sibling:Person)
where type(r1) in ["MOTHER_OF","FATHER_OF"] and type(r2) in ["MOTHER_
OF","FATHER_OF"]
and not(sibling-[:BOUGHT]->prod)
return p.name as Person, prod.name as RecommendedProduct,
collect(sibling.name) as ForSiblings;
```

This would give us the products bought by a specific person, and looks for siblings (who have the same mother or father as the first person) who have not bought that specific product and may potentially benefit from it. Running the query gives us the following result set:

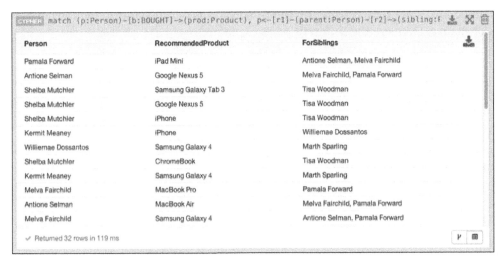

The recommendations based on social ties

Again, a useful recommendation. But now, let's try to bring it all together and really try to make a complex, real-time recommendation based on all of the above criteria: product purchase history, brand loyalty, and social/family networking.

Bringing it all together – compound recommendations

In the following query, we will try to mix all of the three aspects that we mentioned previously into one compound—and hopefully more relevant—recommendation. If we take into account all three angles for our recommendation system, then hopefully we will be able to make fewer, more powerful recommendations to the user. Let's look at the following query:

```
match (p1:Person)-[:BOUGHT]->(prod1:Product)<-[:BOUGHT]-(p2:Person)-
[:BOUGHT]->(prod2:Product), p1<-[r1]-(parent:Person)-[r2]->p2, prod1-
[:MADE_BY]->(br:Brand)<-[:MADE_BY]-(prod2)
where type(r1) in ["MOTHER_OF","FATHER_OF"] and type(r2) in ["MOTHER_
OF","FATHER_OF"] and not(p1-[:BOUGHT]->prod2)
return p1.name as FirstPerson, p2.name as SecondPerson, br.name as
Brand, prod2.name as RecommendedProduct;
```

What we are doing here is bringing the three aspects of our pattern together in the match clause. Here are the different parts explained:

- The first part of the clause ensures that two people have bought common *and* different products

- The second part ensures that the two people are siblings

- The third part ensures that the products recommended would be based on the loyalty to a particular brand

Running this query is interesting. The result is shown in the following screenshot:

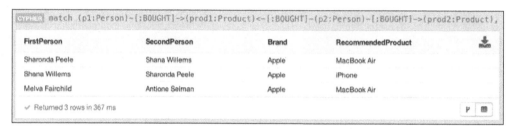

Compound recommendations

We immediately see that we get only three matches to this sophisticated pattern; however, as mentioned earlier, we have reason to believe that these recommendations will be more powerful.

This concludes our discussion of these core use cases around recommendations. Before closing this chapter, we would, however, like to spend a bit more time on some related topics around recommendations.

Business variations on recommendations

The entire principle of a recommender system, as we described before, can be generalized into a different kind of system that has many other business applications. Some people would call it a "rules engine", which does some kind of sophisticated *if-this-then-that* matching and figures out what action to take at the other end of the decision tree. Other people may call it a pattern-matching system, which could be applied to any kind of pattern and tied to any kind of action. Most likely, graph databases such as Neo4j hold some characteristics of all of the above and provide you with an interesting infrastructural optimization that could serve well.

Before wrapping up this chapter, we would like to highlight some use cases that are extremely related to the recommender system use case. Let's go through some well-known sweet spot applications that essentially use the same principles underneath.

Fraud detection systems

We have seen a number of customers that are using Graph Database Management Systems such as Neo4j for fraud detection systems. The principle is quite simple: in many cases, the fraud of a particular nature is not defined by one transaction only, but by a chain of transactions that have their specific characteristics and that need to be compared to one another to see if they really do constitute a case of fraud.

In the following example, we are just looking at a suspect case of credit card fraud:

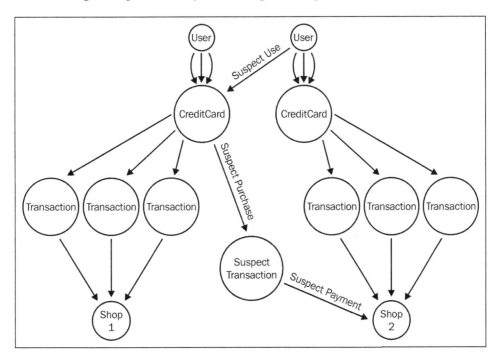

A particular user always uses his credit card for transactions at a particular store. Another user uses his credit card for similar transactions at a different store. And all of a sudden, there is this new transaction in the middle, which uses the credit card (let's say for a similar kind of transaction) in the other store. This kind of pattern may become flagged as a suspect pattern in some fraud detection systems. The system would not necessarily immediately block the credit card, but the risk score of that particular transaction / card combination would definitely go up. If the score reaches a certain threshold, that would mean that there is an increased likelihood for that transaction to be fraudulent, and the system would *recommend* that a particular action be taken.

The action would not be to recommend another product sale, but to put the credit card on hold and give the user a friendly customer service call to check whether this behavioral pattern is exceptional or not. The principle of this fraud detection system, however, would be very similar to that of a retail recommender system: define a pattern, detect a pattern, and act on the occurrence of that pattern with some kind of business-related measure.

Access control systems

Another example of a similar system that uses the principles of a recommender system — defining a pattern and then matching for its occurrences — for a different use case is an access control system.

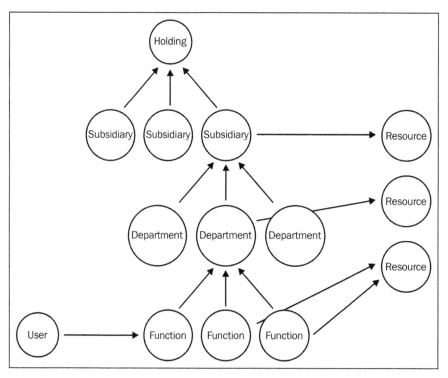

An access graph

Social networking systems

Obviously, there are a lot of recommender systems that will be very specific to a domain. In the past couple of years, with the massive rise of social networking tools and social apps all around us, the interest in social recommender systems has grown massively. Essentially, we are looking to make useful new connections between people that are effectively part of the same social circle, but may not have realized it yet.

Looking at the following sample network should clarify this immediately:

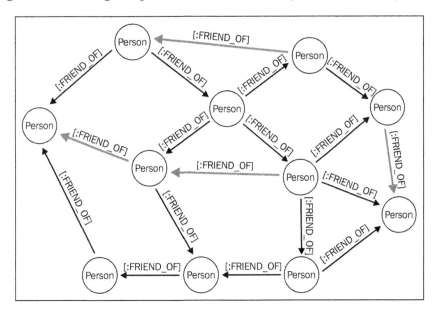

A social networking graph

In the preceding simple network, there is a very high likelihood that we can close some friendship loops very easily, by suggesting connections between new links between people. Very often, we will be using the graph theory principle of *triadic closures*, meaning that we will be closing the missing links of the triangles in the structure of our network.

So let's explore that social networking use case some more in the following chapter with a very specific set of examples.

Questions and answers

Q1: In order to build a recommendation system, I need an artificial intelligence engine that will take a look at my data and discover the recommendation patterns for me automatically.

1. True
2. False

Answer: **False**. Recommender systems can be based on business knowledge that your staff already have, a visual pattern you discover while browsing the data, or some kind of algorithmic machine learning process. All three can provide meaningful recommendation patterns for your business applications.

Q2: Recommender systems can only be applied in an Amazon-style retail environment, where you have a massive amount of data to base your recommendations on.

1. True
2. False

Answer: **False**. Recommendations are useful in many different business domains, not just retail product recommendations. Fraud detection systems (I recommend that you put this person in jail) are just one example of a business application that has nothing to do with retail but that will use the same pattern matching capabilities for detecting these more complicated fraud cases.

Summary

In this chapter, we gave you an overview of how graph databases such as Neo4j could be used in a recommender system. There are a lot of things that we did not discuss, which are out of the scope of this book, but that would probably be part of a true enterprise-class recommender system. Nevertheless, we hope to have illustrated that the querying power of Neo4j will open up a wealth of new opportunities for real-time recommender systems, where recommendations would no longer need to be precalculated but rather leveraged in near real time.

The next chapter will use an example of a use case to teach you about analyzing the impact change has on a process or system. It will also teach you how to analyze impact through graphs.

7
Use Case Example – Impact Analysis and Simulation

In this chapter, we will look at how we can use the Neo4j graph database for another very specific use case: **impact analysis**. All the discussions so far have led us to this discussion, where we really want to zoom in how one would practically use a database such as Neo4j for a very specific use case.

In this chapter, we are going to learn how to perform the following steps:

- Dissect and understand impact analysis systems. We will split the broader topic into two subtopics: impact analysis and impact simulation.

- Apply impact analysis to a Business Process Management use case by using a detailed demonstration dataset.

- Apply impact simulation to a cost calculation use case, using another detailed demonstration dataset.

Let's get started straightaway.

Impact analysis systems dissected

In this chapter, we will spend time with specific types of systems that will allow corporations to perform some of the most complicated operations. In some cases, their information technology infrastructure will be set up to do this, and in others this will not be the case. Analyzing and understanding their businesses in the context of its environment and the impact that the environment has on the business can be tremendously complex. Doing this, in fact, means that companies need to do two very specific things:

- They need to understand how their business will react to specific impulses from the environment or other. Assuming that they have modeled their business as a set of interdependent processes, people, and resources, it is easy to see how graph databases could be very interesting tools to better understand what would happen to the rest of the network if a part of the network changes. We call this the core impact analysis use case.

- They need to be able to simulate different potential scenarios and choose the most optimal scenario to achieve their specific objectives. This, in some sense, becomes a variation of the previously mentioned scenario, but is different in the sense that it requires us to iterate on the previously mentioned scenario many times to determine what would be the optimal end state of the business to achieve the stated objectives. We will call this the impact simulation use case.

Let's now closely examine both of these use cases in some more detail and provide specific examples of both.

Impact analysis in Business Process Management

In the Business Process Management use case, we will be exploring how to use graph database technology to better understand the interdependencies of different business processes and some of their key resources. This is a use case that many large organizations call **Business Process Management**, and is sometimes related to or part of a Business Continuity Management discipline. The idea is plain and simple: if you are a large corporation, and something happens (a natural disaster, a large -scale power outage, a fire, a violent terrorist attack, or any other majorly disruptive event that could hit you as a corporation), then it is essentially your responsibility to prepare for this. The critical step in this preparation process is to understand what depends on what, which is where Neo4j as a graph database comes in to enable that kind of understanding.

Modeling your business as a graph

The example we will use is that of a real-world use case, which combines a number of business concepts that are structured as a graph for better understanding. The concepts are as follows:

- **Business process**: These are the high-level business processes that one would typically consider at a top executive level.
- **Process**: These are composing sub-processes that together make up a business process.
- **Return to Operation Objective**: Both Business processes and their subprocesses will have a maximum timeframe within which they absolutely must return to operation, in case an exceptional event would cause them to suspend operations in the first place. This **Return to Operation Objective (RTO)** can be anything from a few minutes to a few days.
- **Business Line**: Processes will be used by one or more departments or business lines, which are organizational units that should enable the corporation to achieve their objectives.
- **Building**: Business lines are located at a specific site or building.
- **Application**: Processes can use specific Information Technology applications to facilitate their execution.

All of the mentioned concepts are connected to each other, as shown in the following figure:

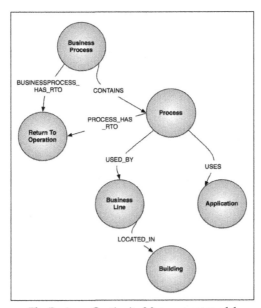

The Business Continuity Management model

We can then easily import a sample dataset into Neo4j. With a simple query, we can see how many relationships we have from a certain type to get some insight in the database:

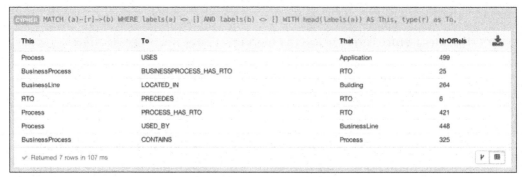

This	To	That	NrOfRels
Process	USES	Application	499
BusinessProcess	BUSINESSPROCESS_HAS_RTO	RTO	25
BusinessLine	LOCATED_IN	Building	264
RTO	PRECEDES	RTO	6
Process	PROCESS_HAS_RTO	RTO	421
Process	USED_BY	BusinessLine	448
BusinessProcess	CONTAINS	Process	325

The BCM database content

The sample dataset in total has 817 nodes and (as you can see from the preceding screenshot) 1988 relationships. This is enough to ask some interesting questions that are appropriate for our use case.

Which applications are used in which buildings

Let's say that we would like to use the graph model to determine which applications are used in specific locations/buildings of our corporation. Then, our Cypher query would look something like the following:

```
MATCH (app:Application)<-[:USES]-(proc:Process)-[:USED_BY]-
>(bl:BusinessLine)-[:LOCATED_IN]->(b:Building)
RETURN DISTINCT app.name AS Application , b.name AS Building
ORDER BY app.name ASC;
```

Note that this is quite an expensive query to run, as it does not use any specific starting points in our graph traversals—it is a global query. However, the result comes back quickly for this dataset:

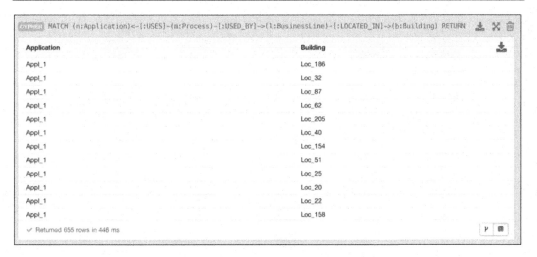

This newfound understanding of the business then allows us to better take action if something would happen to either the application or the building. Let's explore this a bit more.

What buildings are affected if something happens to Appl_9?

This is a very local variety of the preceding query, and it answers the question very specifically for one. The application may be experiencing trouble at this particular moment. The query is similar to the following:

```
MATCH (app:Application {name:"Appl_9"})<-[:USES]-(proc:Process)-
[:USED_BY]->(bl:BusinessLine)-[:LOCATED_IN]->(b:Building)
RETURN DISTINCT app,proc,bl,b;
```

As we have returned the nodes rather than the properties on these nodes, our Neo4j browser returns a nice graphical representation that immediately provides the required insight.

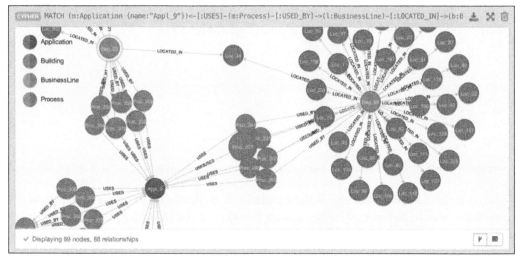

Which buildings are affected if something happens to Appl_9

Hopefully, this is a very good illustration of the use case already, but we can make it a bit more complex by including the RTO information. Let's examine one more query.

What BusinessProcesses with an RTO of 0-2 hours would be affected by a fire at location Loc_100

One thing you would have already noticed is that there is something peculiar about the RTO characteristic. Most people would assume that such a characteristic would become a property of the (business) processes, but in our model, we have created separate nodes to represent these characteristics and linked them together in a chain of RTO values:

- An RTO of 0-2 hours precedes one of 2-4 hours
- An RTO of 2-4 hours precedes one of 4-24 hours
- An RTO of 4-24 hours precedes one of 1-7 days
- An RTO of 1-7 days precedes one of 7-14 days
- And finally, an RTO of 7-14 days precedes on of more than 14 days

You can see this in the following browser graph. The advantage of doing this is that we can now very easily "slide" along the RTO-line and figure out "similar" or "close to" RTO targets very easily.

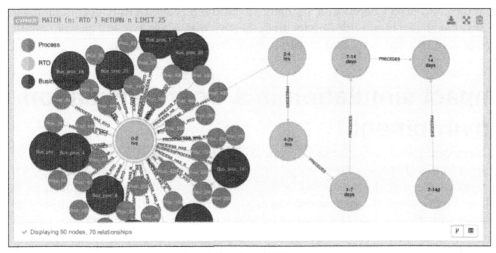

In-graph index of RTO times

So, then we can run the following query to answer the previous question:

```
MATCH (b:Building {name:"Loc_100"}), (rto:RTO {name:"0-2 hrs"})<-
[:BUSINESSPROCESS_HAS_RTO]-(bp:BusinessProcess)
WITH b,bp
MATCH p = ShortestPath(b-[*..3]-bp)
RETURN p;
```

The query uses the `Building` and the `RTO` as starting points for the traversal, and then uses the `ShortestPath` algorithm to find out which business processes would be affected. The result is immediately clear and visible for any business user who wants to analyze the impact of this event on the business environment that the company is operating.

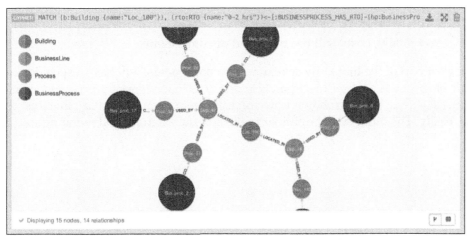

Business processes with RTO affected by incident at location

With these examples behind us, you have a good overview of how graph databases such as Neo4j can help with impact analysis systems . Now, we will explore another type of scenario that is related to this domain: **impact simulation**.

Impact simulation in a Cost Calculation environment

As discussed previously, the second impact-related use case that we would like to address in this chapter is the one that simulates the impact of a certain change to the network on the rest of the network. It basically addresses the "what if" question: how will we be impacted if a certain change occurs in the network? What would be the optimal scenario if we were to change certain parameters in the graph structure?

The example that we will be using in this section uses a very common data structure that you may have seen in many different other use cases: a hierarchy or tree. During the course of this section, we will run through the different parts of tree structure and see what the impact of changes in the tree would be on the rest of the tree.

Modeling your product hierarchy as a graph

The use case that we are exploring uses a hypothetical dataset representing a product hierarchy. This is very common in many manufacturing and construction environments:

- A product is composed of a number of cost groups
- A cost group is composed of a number of cost types
- A cost type is composed of a number of cost subtypes
- A cost subtype is composed of costs
- And finally, costs will be composed of components

The lowest part of the hierarchy structure, the components, will have a specific price. On my blog (http://blog.bruggen.com/2014/03/using-neo4j-to-manage-and -calculate.html), I have shown how you can create a sample dataset like this pretty easily. The model will be similar to the one shown in the following figure:

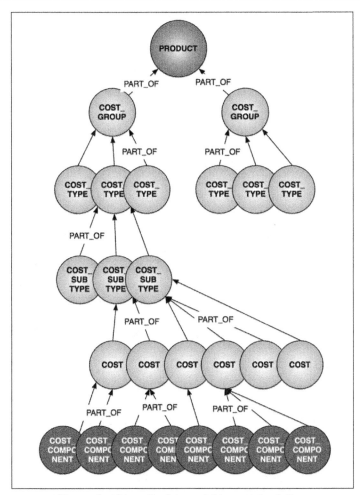

The product hierarchy data model for cost simulations

In our "what if" scenarios that compose our impact simulation, we will be exploring how we can efficiently and easily calculate and recalculate the price of the product if and when the price of one or more of the components changes. Let's get started with this.

Working with a product hierarchy graph

Let's take a look at how we could work with this product hierarchy graph in Neo4j. After adding the data to the graph, we have the following information in our neo4j database:

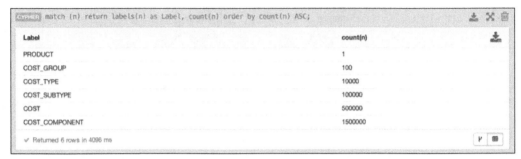

In total, the product hierarchy graph is about 2.1 million nodes and the same number of relationships. This would be a sizeable product hierarchy by any measure. Doing a simple query on the hierarchy reveals the entire top-to-bottom structure:

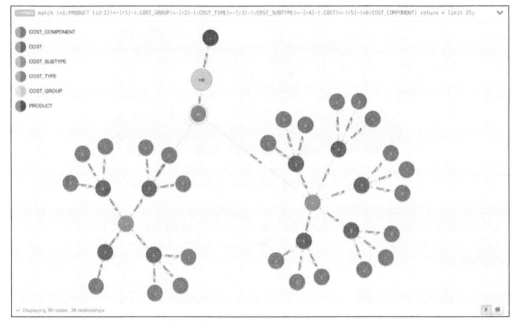

The product hierarchy in Neo4j's browser

Now that we have this hierarchy in place, we can start doing some queries on it. One of the key problems that we would like to solve is the price calculation problem: how do we run through the entire hierarchy structure and use the information stored in the hierarchy to (re)calculate the price of a product? This would typically be a terribly difficult and time-consuming query (as a matter of fact, it is a five-way join operation) on a relational system. So, what would it be on a graph-based database such as Neo4j? Let's find out.

In the following sections, we will actually present two different strategies to calculate the price of the product using the product hierarchy.

The first strategy will be by running through the entire tree, taking the lowest part of the tree for the pricing information and then multiplying that with the quantity information of all the relationships. When this *full sweep* of the tree reaches the top, we will have calculated the entire price of the product.

The second strategy will be using a number of intermediate calculations at every level of the tree. We will update all of the intermediate levels of the tree with the price calculations of everything lying "underneath" it at lower levels of the tree so that, effectively, we would need to run through a much smaller part of the tree to (re)calculate the price.

Let's take a look at this in more detail.

Calculating the price based on a full sweep of the tree

The first strategy we will use to calculate the price of the product in our hierarchy will to a full sweep of the tree:

1. It will start from the product at the top.
2. Then, it will work its way down to every single cost component in the database.
3. Then, it will return the sum of the all total prices, calculated as a product of the price of each cost component with the quantities on the relationships that connect the cost component to the product at the top.

The query for this approach is similar to the following:

```
match
(n1:PRODUCT {id:1})<-[r1]-(:COST_GROUP)<-[r2]-(:COST_TYPE)<-[r3]-
(:COST_SUBTYPE)<-[r4]-(:COST)<-[r5]-(n6:COST_COMPONENT)
return sum(r1.quantity*r2.quantity*r3.quantity*r4.quantity*r5.
quantity*n6.price) as CalculatedPrice;
```

When we execute this query, it takes quite a bit of time, as we need to run through all nodes and relationships of the tree to get what we want. With a tree of 2.1 million nodes and relationships, this took about 47 seconds on my laptop. Look at the result shown in the following screenshot:

Calculating the price based on a full sweep of the hierarchy

Now, anyone who has ever done a similar operation at similar scale in a relational system knows that this is actually a really impressive result. However, we think we can do better by optimizing our hierarchy management strategy and using intermediate pricing information in our queries. If we want to perform impact simulation — the subject of this section of the book — we really want this price calculation to be super fast. So, let's look at that now.

Calculating the price based on intermediate pricing

The strategy optimization that we will be using in this example will be to use intermediate pricing at every level of the tree. By doing so, we will enable our price calculation to span a much smaller part of the graph, that is, only the part of the graph that changes — the node/relationship that changes and everything "above" it in the hierarchy — will need to be traversed when performing our impact simulations.

To do so, we need to add that intermediate pricing information to the hierarchy. Currently, only the lowest cost component level has pricing information. Also, we need to calculate that information for all levels of the hierarchy. We use a query similar to the following one to do so:

```
match (n5:COST)<-[r5]-(n6:COST_COMPONENT)
with n5, sum(r5.quantity*n6.price) as Sum
set n5.price=Sum;
```

Essentially, what we do is we look at one level of the hierarchy, traverse upwards to the level above, and set the price of the upper level equal to the sum of all products of the price of the lower level and multiplied by the quantity of the relationship that connects it to the upper level.

As previously mentioned, we need to run that type of query for every level of our hierarchy:

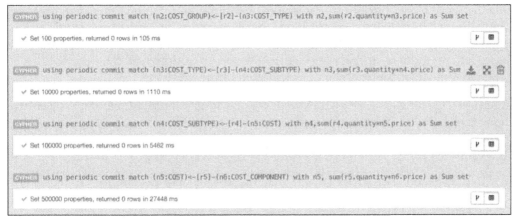

Adding intermediate pricing information

About 35 seconds later, this is all done, which is quite impressive.

Now that we have the intermediate pricing information, calculating the price of the product only needs to traverse one level deep. We use a query similar to the following one:

```
match (n1:PRODUCT {id:1})<-[r1]-(n2:COST_GROUP)
return sum(r1.quantity*n2.price);
```

Of course, this query is significantly faster, as it only touches a hundred or so nodes and relationships — instead of 2.1 million of each. So, note the super-fast query that yields an identical result to the full sweep of the tree mentioned previously:

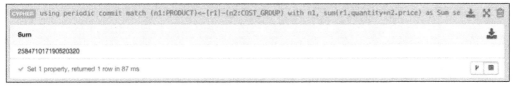

Calculating price based on intermediate pricing

Now that we have done this optimization once, we can use this mechanism for our impact simulation queries.

Impact simulation on product hierarchy

Our original objective was all about impact simulation. We want to understand what happens to the price of the product at the top of our product hierarchy by simulating what happens if one or more cost component price changes. If this simulation would be sufficiently performant, then we could probably iterate on these changes quite frequently and use it as a way to optimize all the processes dependent on an appropriate price calculation of the product.

In the new, optimized strategy that we have previously outlined, we can very easily change the price of a cost component (at the bottom of the hierarchy), and as we update that price, recalculate all the intermediate prices that are set at the levels above the cost component (cost, cost subtype, cost type, cost group, and finally, the product). Let's look at the following query (which consists of multiple parts):

Part	Query

Part 1	```match (n6:COST_COMPONENT)```
	```with n6, n6.price as OLDPRICE limit 1```
	```set n6.price = n6.price*10```
	```with n6.price-OLDPRICE as PRICEDIFF,n6```

Part 2	```match n6-[r5:PART_OF]->(n5:COST)-[r4:PART_OF]-```
	```>(n4:COST_SUBTYPE)-[r3:PART_OF]->(n3:COST_TYPE)-```
	```[r2:PART_OF]->(n2:COST_GROUP)-[r1:PART_OF]-```
	```(n1:PRODUCT)```

Part 3	```set n5.price=n5.price+(PRICEDIFF*r5.quantity),```
	```n4.price=n4.price+(PRICEDIFF*r5.quantity*r4.```
	```quantity),```
	```n3.price=n3.price+(PRICEDIFF*r5.quantity*r4.```
	```quantity*r3.quantity),```
	```n2.price=n2.price+(PRICEDIFF*r5.quantity*r4.```
	```quantity*r3.quantity*r2.quantity),```
	```n1.price=n1.price+(PRICEDIFF*r5.quantity*r4.```
	```quantity*r3.quantity*r2.quantity*r1.quantity)```
	```return PRICEDIFF, n1.price;```

- **Part 1**: This looks up the price of one single cost component, changes it by multiplying it by 10, and then passes the difference between the new price and the old price (`PRICEDIFF`) to the next part of the query.

- **Part 2**: This climbs the tree to the very top of the hierarchy and identifies all of the parts of the hierarchy that will be affected by the change executed in Part 1.

- **Part 3**: This uses the information of Part 1 and Part 2, and recalculates and sets the price at every intermediate level that it passes. At the top of the tree (n1), it will return the new price of the product.

Running this query on the dataset runs the following result:

Recalculating the price with one change in the hierarchy

This is really good; recalculating the price over a hierarchy of 2.1 million things all of a sudden only takes 117 milliseconds. Not too bad. Let's see if that also works if we change the price of more than one cost component. If we use the preceding query but change limit 1 to limit 100 and run this query, we get the following result:

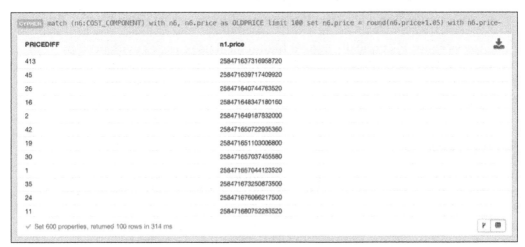

Recalculating the price based on 100 changes in the hierarchy

The effect of recalculating the price of the product based on a hundred changes in the hierarchy is done in 314 milliseconds — a truly great result. This sets us up for a fantastic way of *simulating these impacts* over our dataset.

This concludes our discussion of the impact simulation and allows us to start wrapping up this chapter.

Questions and Answers

Q1. Analyzing impact often requires:

1. A lot of manual work in the database.

2. Complex join operations across multiple different types of information.

3. A simple path finding query over a graph database such as Neo4j.

A: 3. Path finding is a great use case for Neo4j.

Q2. Which of the following use cases is a great hierarchical use case for Neo4j?

1. Calculating the average selling price over a million different purchase transactions.

2. Calculating access control over a directory tree of users in groups and departments.

3. Calculating the shortest path on a road network between two cities.

4. Recommending a new product purchase to an existing client.

A: 2. Access control is typically a great hierarchical use case, as evidenced by }the multiple hierarchically organized directory servers on the market today. Hierarchies, however, are just a specific type of graph and so they are typically also a great use case for Neo4j.

Summary

In this chapter, we illustrated that graph databases such as Neo4j are extremely well placed at playing a role in many enterprise architectures where impact analysis and simulation would be important. There are many different fields where this may be useful, but we chose two specific domains to illustrate this use case. First, we took a look at a Business Process Management use case, where analyzing and understanding the potential impact of a change in a network would be of primary interest to the user. Then, we took a look at an impact simulation use case, where we wanted to set up a use case in which we would want to iteratively simulate different impact scenarios and see what would be the result of those changes on the network, using a product hierarchy as an example to do so.

We hope to have given you a good overview of the use cases and its potential. We will now continue to the next chapter of this book, which deals with graphical visualizations for Neo4j.

8
Visualizations for Neo4j

In this chapter, we will look at the fascinating domain of graph visualizations within the context of the Neo4j Graph Database Management System. We will go into the reasons why these kinds of visualizations can be so wonderfully important, discuss different technical tools to help you with these visualizations, and then finally discuss some of the common do's and don'ts within this domain.

In this chapter, we will discuss the following topics:

- The power of visualizations, and graph visualizations more specifically
- The basic principles and components of a graph visualization solution
- Different visualization libraries and solutions on the market today for your use

With that, let's dive right in.

The power of graph visualizations

In this section, we will spend time discussing the reasons why graph visualizations are so important, and highlight some of the underpinning technologies that are used in the different solutions that we will zoom into later on.

Why graph visualizations matter!

There are many reasons why the graph visualizations that we will discuss in this chapter, as well as the ones that we have previously seen and will show hereafter, are really nice. But for a limited number of reasons, they are more than nice: they matter greatly, and can have a massive impact on decisions being made, big or small. Let's discuss these.

Interacting with data visually

From a very early age, we are taught to interact with data in a cognitive way—focused on analysis, not understanding. We are not supposed or encouraged to look at data in a creative, fun, or interesting way that induces insight. This, however, is now changing. There's an entirely new discipline emerging in the field of data science and analytics, which stresses the visual aspects of interacting with data. Visual interaction, as opposed to cognitive interaction, tends to have some qualities for average human beings who do not have the technical or scientific background that some people may have. By extension, many different business managers may also find this new way of interaction quite interesting. Here are some reasons why:

- It allows people to extract key information at a glance. In an age of sub-second attention spans and massive information overload, this can be truly important to get a point across and help your audience sift through what is and what is not important.

- We all know the cliché: a picture says more than a thousand words. The reason it is a cliché, of course, is that it is true. Pictures are usually easier to understand, and perhaps more importantly, also easier to remember.

Edward Tufte's reference work on visualization

We could expand on both points quite elaborately, but instead we are going to recommend that you read up on books like Edward R. Tufte's for more details. It is sufficient to say that graph visualizations can be truly powerful, and that most Neo4j projects today will have some kind of visualization component to them for a combination of the previously stated reasons.

Looking for patterns

Expanding on and adding to the previous points on visualization, there is another great reason for interacting with Neo4j in a visual way. The fact is that graph visualizations allow humans to really use an otherwise underused capacity of our brains: pattern recognition. When we interact with data in the traditional way (through lists of things, tabular structured reports, and summary statistics), it is very difficult for our brain to discern any kind of pattern. We would need to read, assimilate, and cognitively process all data before anything like that would become possible. But in graph visualization, in many cases, we can just leverage the primal capability that we have built into our machinery: the ability to recognize patterns. Pattern recognition is a key capability of the human brain, and one we should leverage and exploit in our business life. Representing data in a visual way, like in a graph visualization, is a natural thing for us to do—and can yield very powerful results. After all, that's why we whiteboard, mindmap, or doodle when we work and discuss with our colleagues, isn't it?

Spot what's important

Part of the power of these results will be in being able to separate the wheat from the chaff and find out what is truly important in a particular data set. Sometimes, that *important* piece will be in the density of the connections between a particular data entity and the other entities. Sometimes, it will be more in the intensity of the connections. And at other times, it will be the outliers that will be the more important data elements—the ones with limited amounts of connectivity with the rest of the data structure. Those data elements, which at a minimum will be interesting if not important, will jump out of a graph visualization immediately, whereas they may never surface in a long list of data elements that we could easily glance over.

For all of the mentioned reasons, graph visualization is truly important and should definitely be examined in detail by anyone interested in doing a Neo4j graph database project.

The basic principles of graph visualization

In order to visualize a graph structure, we need to take into account a number of aspects. Like with any visualization, it is very easy to let the trees disappear into the forest—in graphs, we often talk about the *hairball* effect. Connected structures such as graphs can very easily become very unclear and opaque to the user; it takes a couple of very well-defined mechanisms to lay out the graph to the user in an intelligible way. More specifically, we tend to find three main mechanisms that are used by different technology solutions that we will treat later on. Let's go through these mechanisms.

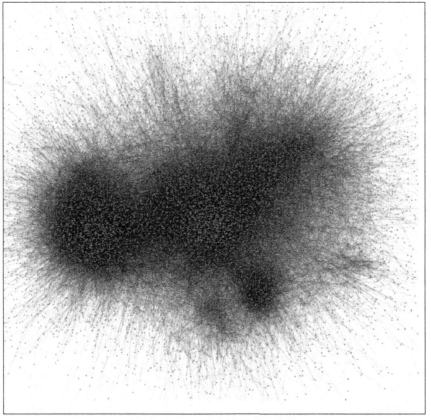

Graphs can quickly look like hairballs

 Before doing so, I want to specifically thank my friend and colleague Alistair Jones for his insightful talks that gave me many of the ideas presented in this section. Please visit www.apcjones.com if you want to learn more.

Here are the three mechanisms to keep in mind:

- **Gravity**: In order for a graph visualization to make sense to a user, things that belong together need to be presented together. These items will need to gravitate to one another using some kind of force that will be calculated based on the characteristics of the nodes and relationships that will be stored in the Neo4j database management system.

- **Charge**: By the same logic, there needs to be a force that keeps items apart from one another. We call this **charge**, as we know from a long-forgotten course in school that substances with a similar positive or negative charge will repel each other. Similarly, we will associate a charge to different items in the graph to keep them from overlapping and make sure that they are visualized apart.

- **Springs**: As with many other data visualization solutions, it helps the effectiveness of the graph visualization greatly if the solution is presented in a dynamic and vivid fashion. In a graph database visualization like the ones that we want to hook up to Neo4j, this often means that we would appreciate some kind of springy behavior that displays the data in a way that is not as static as usual but that moves around on the screen as it is built or as it is manipulated by the user. The spring analogy aims to explain that we will appreciate the type of visualization that will go back and forth a bit before it stabilizes on the screen.

With these three underlying techniques, a number of very interesting visualization libraries and full-fledged solutions have been built. We will take the next couple of sections to highlight these briefly so that you know where you can find some potential components of your Neo4j solution.

Open source visualization libraries

Many developers that use Neo4j as their Graph Database Management System end up having some very specific needs to visualize the network and present that to their end users in an integrated way as part of their application. These Neo4j users, who are typically not afraid of getting their hands dirty with some code, will typically like to build that visualization using a library of tools that fit their purpose. There are several tools out there that could be used, so let's give you a little overview of the most popular ones.

D3.js

D3, pronounced "dee three", is another way to refer to a library that is supposed to enable and provide data-driven documents. It is a JavaScript library for manipulating documents based on data. You can find the latest version on `www.d3js.org`. D3 helps you visualize data using HTML, SVG, and CSS. D3's emphasis on web standards gives you the full capabilities of modern browsers without tying yourself to a proprietary framework, combining powerful visualization components and a data-driven approach to the manipulation of the **Document Object Model (DOM)** that is the basis of HTML and XML documents.

As such, D3.js is not limited to the visualization of graphs—it aims to solve the heart of many data visualization problems: being able to manipulate a dataset interactively based on some kind of document. Once that is solved, the data can be manipulated independent of the format or representation, which offers great flexibility and has made the D3 libraries very popular with developers, and which is why many other libraries are built on top of it.

D3 visualization of a graph

Graphviz

Graphviz is an open source graph visualization software that you can download from www.graphviz.org. It is often quoted as being the granddaddy of visualization software, but is still very actively used and developed. It provides several main layout programs and also features web and interactive graphical interfaces, as well as helper tools, libraries, and language bindings. The core Graphviz team claims not to be able to put a lot of work into GUI editors, but there are quite a few external projects and even commercial tools that incorporate Graphviz.

The Graphviz layout programs take descriptions of graphs in a simple text language and create diagrams in useful formats, for example, images and SVG for web pages and PDF or Postscript for inclusion in other documents or display in an interactive graph browser.

Graphviz has many useful features for concrete diagrams, such as options for colors, fonts, tabular node layouts, line styles, hyperlinks, and custom shapes.

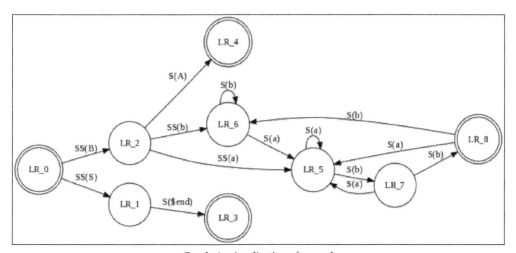

Graphviz visualisation of a graph

Sigma.js

Sigma is a JavaScript library dedicated to graph drawing. You can find it on `www.sigmajs.org`. It makes it easy to publish networks on web pages and allows developers to integrate network exploration in rich web applications. Sigma provides a lot of built-in features that are optimized for modern browsers, such as Canvas and WebGL renderers or mouse and touch support. This is supposed to make network manipulation on web pages smooth and fast for the user.

Sigma provides a lot of different settings to make it easy to customize drawing and interaction with networks. And you can also directly add your own functions to your scripts to render nodes and edges the exact way you want. Sigma is a rendering engine, and it is up to you to add all the interactivity you want. The public API makes it possible to modify the data, move the camera, refresh the rendering, listen to events, and many other things. It's probably for some of these reasons that the visualization solution of Linkurio.us, which we will come back to later in this chapter, uses sigma.js under the hood.

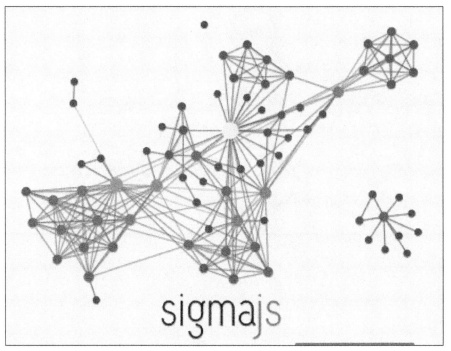

Sigma.js visualization of a graph

Vivagraph.js

Vivagraph is a free and fast graph drawing library for JavaScript. It is designed to be extensible and to support different rendering engines and layout algorithms. You can download the most recent version from `https://github.com/anvaka/VivaGraphJS` and see some very nice demos of it at `www.yasiv.com`. At the moment, it supports rendering graphs using WebGL, SVG, or CSS formats. The author Andrei Kashcha is also working on a more modular and extensible library called Ngraph; you can find details of it on `https://github.com/anvaka/ngraph`.

Some of the vivagraph.js examples on Yasiv are a lot of fun to use, and powerfully illustrate that graphs can be used very well for things such as recommendations: it takes a split-second view of the Amazon recommendation graph to understand how one might use this. Have a look at the following screenshot:

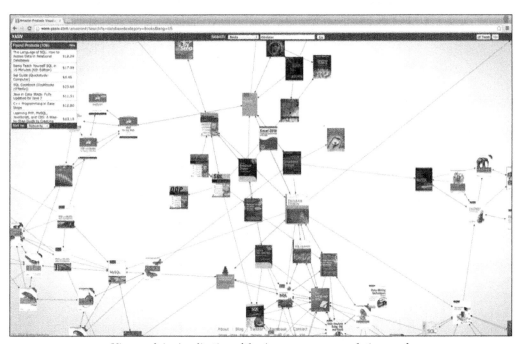

Vivagraph.js visualization of the Amazon recommendation graph

Those were probably some of the more popular open source visualization libraries out there.

Integrating visualization libraries in your application

Integrating libraries will always follow a similar pattern, as illustrated by the following figure:

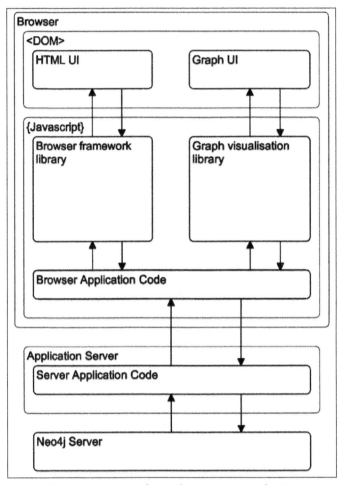

How to integrate graph visualizations in an application

The browser will contain two parts:

- The **DOM**, with the actual data. This contains the graph data as part of the total web page.
- The **JavaScript** part, with the browser framework as well as the graph visualization library (one of the ones mentioned before, possibly) and perhaps some other application code.

The application server will be on the other end of the Internet connection to provide the application interface to the user. This server will typically have some business logic hosted on it, but will most probably also have to integrate with a database management system like Neo4j.

The Neo4j server in the back will be serving up result sets based on queries generated by the aforementioned business logic.

This architecture allows us to understand how any of these libraries would need to be hooked into our application. With that, we will now turn our attention to some more packaged visualization solutions that can be used in combination with Neo4j.

Visualization solutions

We make a distinction between visualization libraries and visualization solutions for a very specific reason: they serve very different purposes.

Many members of the Neo4j user community have been developing their own application-specific visualization applications that are typically very customized. They aim to solve a very specific visualization problem, and use a library to do so, because it allows them to tweak the visualization to their liking at the expense of a bit more work.

There are, however, also those users of the Neo4j Graph Database Management System that require a more general, less optimized but more readily available visualization solution. For those users, visualization "solutions" are a better option, as they are typically readily available, off-the-shelf solutions that require little or no customization to start adding value. These are the solutions that we will be discussing in this section of our book. So, let's take a look.

Note that we will be discussing these solutions in alphabetical order; there is no preference or order displayed in these pages, as we firmly believe that most of these tools are very complementary to one another.

Gephi

Gephi is an interactive visualization and exploration platform for all kinds of networks and complex systems, dynamic graphs, and hierarchical graphs. It is developed by the Gephi Consortium, a not-for-profit legal entity in France created to ensure future developments of Gephi. They aim to develop a number of tools in an open source ecosystem, focused on the visualization and analysis of large networks in real-time. Their tagline, *Like Photoshop but for data*, gives you a good feel of what they want to do: Gephi helps data analysts intuitively reveal patterns and trends, highlight outliers, and tell stories with their data.

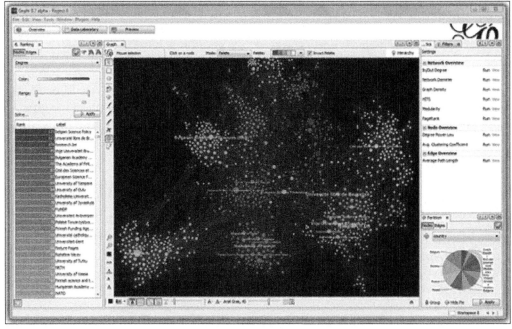

Gephi graph visualization and analysis

The toolset runs on Windows, Linux, and Mac OS X and has a very extensible architecture that, for example, allows you to import and export Neo4j databases.

What makes Gephi interesting from my perspective is its capability to do both graph visualization and, at least for small-to-medium sized graphs, graph analytics. It can be of great help in discovering new patterns in your data—even those patterns that you are currently not aware of.

Keylines

UK-based startup Cambridge Intelligence (`http://cambridge-intelligence.com/`) has been building a very interesting toolkit for graph visualization called Keylines (`http://keylines.com/`) that has been gaining traction quite quickly in the law enforcement, fraud detection, counter terrorism, CRM, sales, and social network data sectors.

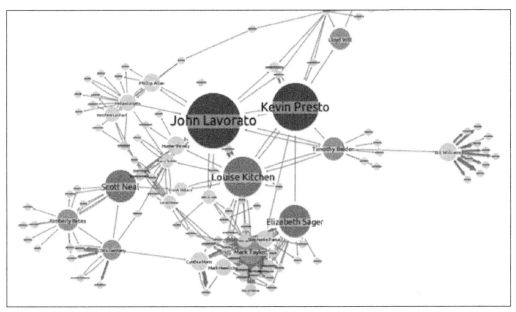

Keylines graph visualization

Keylines is interesting in many different ways from a technical perspective, mostly because it can be deployed on any browser or device without too much difference in architecture and support. It allows for both standard out-of-the-box deployment, as well as deep customization using the System Development Kit that is provided with their commercial licenses.

Linkurio.us

Linkurio.us (http://linkurio.us/) is probably one of the more interesting and newer additions to the graph visualization landscape. It was started in France by some of Gephi's original founders and contributors. They now offer a very well-rounded, moderately priced, easily accessible entry point for people that want an advanced graph visualization toolkit without having to jump through the hoops of building one.

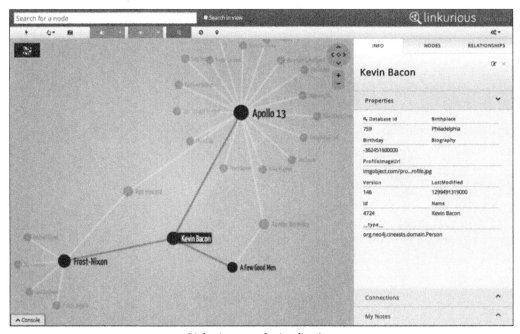

Linkurio.us graph visualization

Linkurio.us is a very nice alternative for graph visualizations, offering a packaged solution with lots of interesting features and a plug-and-play installation on top of an existing Neo4j database management system.

Neo4j Browser

With the arrival of Neo4j 2.0 in late 2013, the team at Neo Technology provided an entirely new way of interacting with graph data, entirely based on an intuitive way to interact with the graph database using Cypher. This environment, called Neo4j Browser, is a bit of a hybrid between a data query tool and a development environment. It provides many of the tools that one would expect to use in an interactive exploration of graph data, allows for saving of queries and visual styling, and is gradually being expanded with more and more functionality.

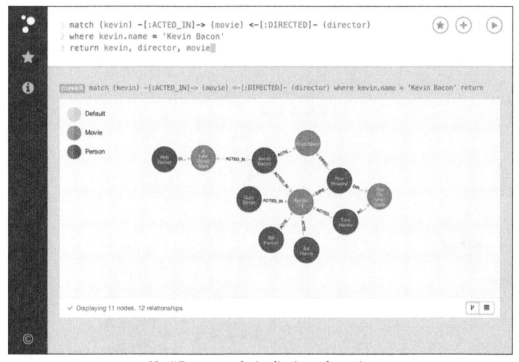

Neo4j Browser graph visualization and querying

Neo4j Browser is, at the time of this writing, still under constant development, with new features being constantly added. One of the interesting new developments now is that Neo Technology will actually allow for the extraction and embedding of browser visualization functionality into your own applications.

Tom Sawyer

One of the lesser known alternatives for graph visualization, at least in Europe, is Tom Sawyer Software's *Perspectives* line of products. Look at `https://www.tomsawyer.com` for the company's website and `https://www.tomsawyer.com/products/perspectives/index.php` for more information on Perspectives.

This is an advanced graphics-based software for building enterprise-class data relationship visualization and analysis applications. It features a complete **Software Development Kit** (**SDK**) with a graphics-based design and preview environment that lets you build, test, and deploy graph visualizations more easily, based on a reference architecture.

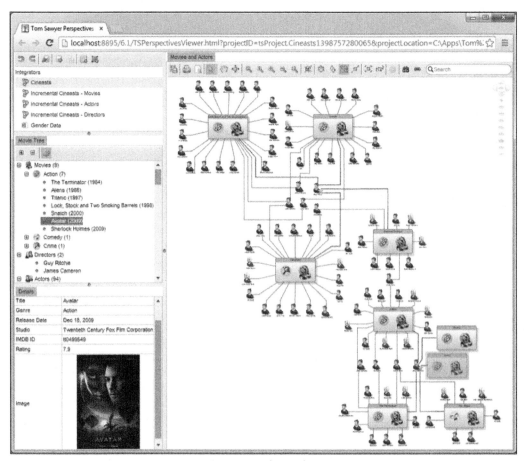

Tom Sawyer graph visualization

Tom Sawyer also offers standard data integration capabilities for Neo4j's Graph Database Management System.

With that, we are close to wrapping up the chapter on graph visualizations of this book. We do have a couple of closing remarks that we would like to add before we move on.

Closing remarks on visualizations

It should be clear by now that once we have our data models in a Graph Database Management System like Neo4j, one of the great potential use cases for that system is tightly coupled to visualization capabilities. It is amazing what we can learn from visualizations, but we do want to point out two caveats that you should always be keeping in mind as you engage in a visualization project.

The "fireworks" effect

While graph visualizations usually have a very positive effect on its users, we—as IT people that are provided this as an interface to interact with data—must also be aware of the fact that these visualizations can be a bit too much sometimes. We call that the "fireworks" effect, and while by no means specific to graph visualizations, it is an important thing to be aware of. The purpose of visualization can never be to attract oooohs and aaaahs—that's what fireworks are supposed to do for the crowds of spectators that they attract. Contrarily, the purpose of visualization should always be to communicate with the beholders and to transfer information from the software application that we are building on top of a Graph Database Management System such as Neo4j to its users. This seems like a trivial point, but we know from experience that it is often forgotten.

The "loading" effect

With that purpose of visualizations in mind, we should also take into account another aspect that is crucially important in the world of data visualizations: the loading effect. This effect is, again, not specific to graph visualizations and is omnipresent in many charts and graphics presented by newspapers and television reports alike. We mean to highlight the effect that a particular type of presentation of the data has in the interpretation process of the user.

By making certain choices on how we present the data, the options that we present to the user, even the colors that we choose for certain data elements, we may load the visualization with certain expectations and interpretations on behalf of the end user. Data visualizations should therefore always highlight and explain the choices made to the end user and offer different ways of representing the data if that would be of use.

Questions and answers

Q1. If I wanted to build an application that included graph visualization, I would have to build that visualization from scratch.

1. True
2. False

A. False. While many applications benefit from a customized visualization solution, there are a number of solutions and libraries out there that can help you. At a minimum, these libraries and/or solutions will provide you with a baseline from which you can start.

Q2. The three basic graph visualization forces used in many tools are:

1. Gravity, Obesity, Charge
2. Springs, Gravity, Charge
3. Charge, Gravity, Verbosity

A. Springs, Gravity, Charge.

Q3. The well-know effect of data visualizations containing too much information, so much so that the user gets confused and cannot see the wood for the trees, is often referred to as:

1. The forest effect
2. The loading effect
3. The fireworks effect

A. The fireworks effect.

Summary

We conclude our chapter on graph visualization. In this chapter, we went through the reasons why graph visualizations matter greatly to modern-day data applications. We also illustrated different tools and techniques that could be used by application developers to create their graph database applications. We then wrapped up the chapter by pointing out some very important side effects of visualization solutions, and how we could take these effects into account when we engage in such a project.

The next chapter will cover topics to teach you to import data into Neo4j. You will learn about the tools that can be used to import this data into your databases.

Other Tools Related to Neo4j

9

No database is complete without some tooling around it. Developers and database administrators alike need additional tools — besides the database proper — to make the database fit into a more holistic solution. Neo4j as a Graph Database Management System is no different in that respect. In this chapter, we would like to point out some important tools that are related to Neo4j and can be important in specific user environments. More specifically, we will look at:

- Data integration tools
- Business Intelligence tools
- Modeling tools

No doubt there are other tools that could be of use, but this should get you started.

Data integration tools

Very often, users will want to use the Neo4j Graph Database as part of a solution that uses a **polyglot persistence** strategy. This is a term that was first coined by Scott Leberknight, but later used and explained many times by well-known authors such as Martin Fowler. Essentially, what we are talking about here is the fact that most complex applications these days feature a number of different data patterns that are used under very different workloads and that can therefore benefit from very different implementation strategies.

Here's what a potential polyglot persistence architecture could look like for a hypothetical, or speculative, retailer:

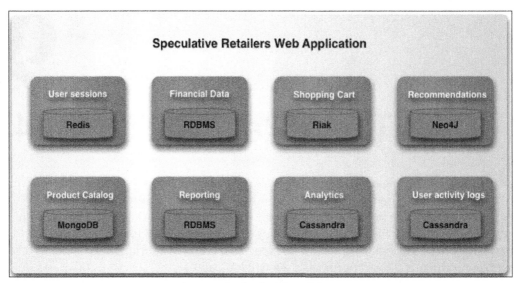

An example of polyglot persistence

In the **Speculative Retailer's Web Application** featured in the preceding figure, there may be different use cases that rely on different data patterns, and that would be best implemented in different data stores.

The consequence of a strategy like polyglot persistence is, of course, that you introduce the immediate and significant need for data integration. Different Data Integration strategies are of course conceivable, but at least one of these will rely on third-party tooling to read from and write to the Neo4j Graph Database Management System. Therefore, we would like to introduce two examples of tools like these and discuss their characteristics and potential use cases.

Talend

Talend (www.talend.com) is an open source software vendor that provides Data Integration, data management, enterprise application integration, and Big Data software and services. They have a very extensible, visual, and powerful development environment for all kinds of integration services that can all be connected together in a workflow designer-style environment.

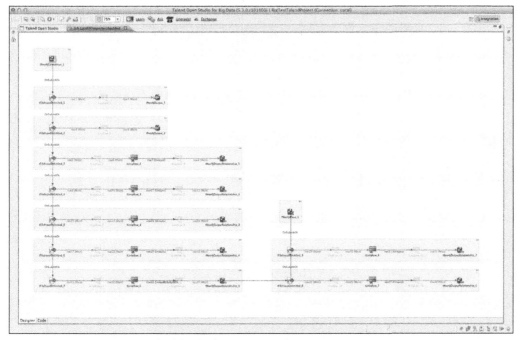

Talend Studio for Big Data with Neo4j connectivity

The Talend toolset is definitely very interesting for Neo4j users to take a look at. The original connector for Neo4j was developed by Zenika, a French system integrator, but was afterwards integrated in the core toolset of Talend Open Studio for Big Data, the Talend Enterprise Big Data, and Talend Platform for Big Data products. At the time of writing, the connector has been lagging behind Neo4j releases a little bit, but has been sufficiently powerful in usability and technical proficiency that it deserves a recommendation in this section of our book.

MuleSoft

MuleSoft (www.mulesoft.com), headquartered in San Francisco, California, provides an integration platform to connect any application, datasource, or API, whether in the cloud or on-premises. Just like Talend, it offers a visual environment to integrate other datasources in the polyglot persistence architecture with the Neo4j graph database management system. To do so, MuleSoft provides a well-documented connector for Neo4j that allows you to integrate very easily.

The MuleSoft Neo4j connector

The MuleSoft connector offers a connectivity metaphor that is a bit similar to what LOAD CSV and the Neo4j shell tools provide, in that they allow you to use variables (read from incoming data streams that can come from different alternative data sources) to include in Cypher statements. It is very easy to understand and use if you are already a bit familiar with Cypher, which is probably the case by now.

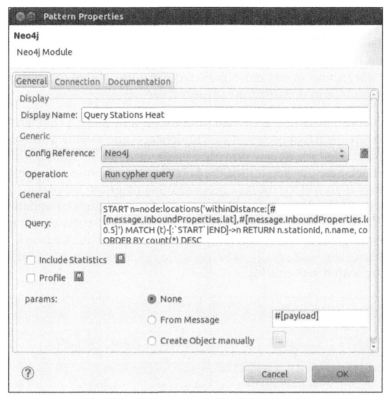

Sending a Cypher query to Neo4j via MuleSoft

The MuleSoft toolset also seems to be well documented and well maintained, providing developers with a stable platform for their integration applications.

Business Intelligence tools

Because Neo4j as a graph database management system provides many advantages when interacting with inherently networked and interconnected data structures, many traditional data analysis tools can benefit greatly from leveraging its query power. There is, most notably, an entire category of tools out there that are a prime candidate for doing so: the so-called *Business Intelligence* tools. Tools in this space include (but are certainly not limited to):

- IBM Cognos
- SAP Business Objects
- Pentaho
- Jaspersoft
- Qlikview

We will zoom into one of these tools in the following paragraphs, but would first like to clarify the mechanism through which these tools can interface with Neo4j. Of course, they could integrate by calling the raw Neo4j REST API and submittin specific requests this way, and would get responses in the rawest possible format. This type of integration would most likely require quite a bit of integration work, but could be advised in certain more advanced use cases.

There are, however, many use cases that can be solved by using a standardized integration mechanism that is overall well understood and readily available: most of the tools mentioned previously provide a mechanism for integrating with a standardized database interface called the **Java Database Connectivity interface**. This technology is an API for the Java programming language that defines how a client may access a database. It provides methods for querying and updating data in a database. By default, JDBC is oriented towards relational databases, but luckily for our discussion, a great deal of work has gone into a JDBC driver for Neo4j. You can download this driver from `http://www.neo4j.org/develop/tools/jdbc` and start experimenting with it very quickly.

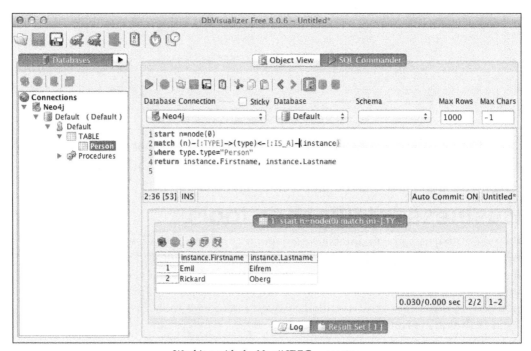

Working with the Neo4j JDBC connector

As you can see from the preceding screenshot, you can write Neo4j queries in Cypher, send them over the wire via the JDBC driver to Neo4j, and receive the result set in a standardized tabular format. This format can then be used by tools like the Business Intelligence tools mentioned previously and integrated in their capabilities.

A very good case study of such an integration is provided by the way Qlikview integrates with Neo4j. Developed by a German company called TIQ Solutions (`http://www.tiq-solutions.de/`), it provides a full and comprehensive solution for integrating Neo4j with the Qlikview Business Intelligence suite of applications.

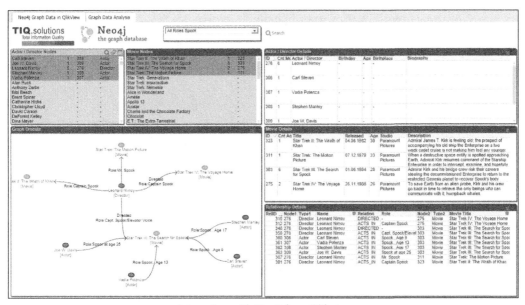

Integrating with Neo4j from Qlikview

All of these integrations make use of a JDBC connectivity that can be tuned to the Qlikview application development environment. For more information, you can visit `http://www.tiq-solutions.de/display/enghome/ENJDBC` and `http://tiqview.tumblr.com/`. The Neo4j website also features a number of links to examples and case studies that could be of use.

The mechanism outlined earlier, using the JDBC connectivity provided by Neo4j's driver, is a very powerful integration mechanism that can combine the best of the other worlds and can make the query power of graph databases such as Neo4j available to a broader user audience.

Modeling tools

As we saw in *Chapter 4, Modeling Data for Neo4j*, modeling for Graph databases is just as important as ever. Even though there is no external schema overlooking our data model by default, there is still a clear and important need to model. The way to define the structure of the data that we are planning to store in Neo4j needs to be documented in a clear and understandable fashion. In this section of our book, we will outline two frequently used tools that we can suggest for the development of our graph models:

- The homegrown open source toolset developed by Alistair Jones and GraphAlchemist, appropriately called Arrows
- The commercially developed and supported toolset of OmniGraffle

Let's provide a bit more detail on each of these tools.

Arrows

Originally started by Neo Technology's, Alistair Jones (www.apcjones.com) as a side project for graph documentation and visualization, the Arrows toolset today enables very easy and useable documentation of graph database models. The tool is available online at www.apcjones.com/arrows and provides very basic but advanced graph drawing capabilities.

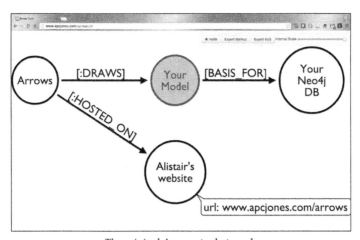

The original Arrows tool at work

The nicest thing about the Arrows model is that it enables exact mapping of the property graph model of Neo4j onto the drawing canvas. Its automatic scaling and alignment features are also extremely useful.

The Arrows toolset, which is an open source project publicly available on `https://github.com/apcj/arrows`, was subsequently adopted and forked by the team at `www.graphalchemist.com` and enriched with a new data format (based on JSON instead of XML) and coloring possibilities.

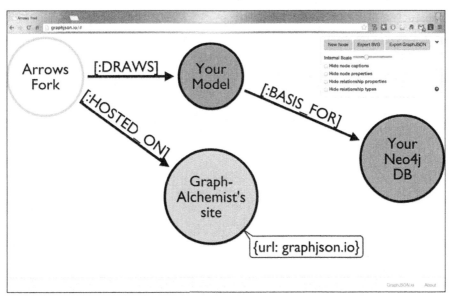

The forked graphjson tool at work

You can find the documentation on `www.graphjson.org`, the code on `https://github.com/GraphAlchemist/GraphJSON`, and a working example on `www.graphjson.io` for you to play with.

Now, we can turn our attention to a better-rounded modeling tool that has been around for years, and provides lots of mature capabilities: OmniGraffle.

OmniGraffle

OmniGraffle (http://www.omnigroup.com/omnigraffle/) is a diagramming application made by The Omni Group (http://www.omnigroup.com/). OmniGraffle is built only for Mac OS X and iPad. It may be used to create diagrams, flow charts, org charts, illustrations, and graph database models. It features a drag-and-drop WYSIWYG interface. **Stencils** — groups of shapes to drag-and-drop — are available as extensions for OmniGraffle, and users can create their own stencils, for example, to get easy access to property graph editing requirements. In many of these respects, OmniGraffle is similar to Microsoft Visio.

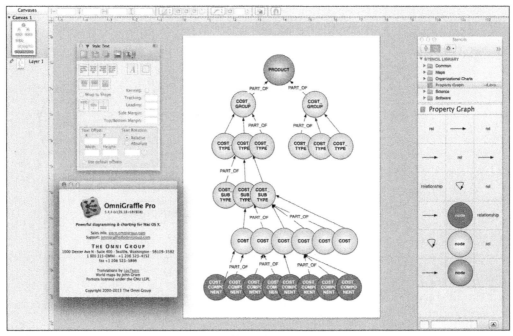

The OmniGraffle modeling tool at work

Having used OmniGraffle for a number of models, I believe that it provides excellent capabilities to draw larger and more complex models. The multilayer capabilities and rich drawing palettes allow you to integrate the model into broader documents that can be used for other purposes as well. The only major negative aspect at this point seems to be its limited support for the Windows platform.

With that, we have covered the important tooling additions that we wanted to provide to our book and are ready to wrap up.

Questions and answers

Q1. What programming language is used to interact with Data Integration tools like Talend and MuleSoft to accomplish our Neo4j integrations?

1. Any programming language can be used
2. You have to use Java
3. You do not need to develop—you can use visual development tools to achieve the integration
4. Java is supported, but Erlang is preferred

A. You do not need to develop—you can use visual development tools to achieve the integration

Q2. What is the major downside of using OmniGraffle for developing graph database models?

1. It does not integrate with the database natively
2. You need to use a drawing tablet to use the software
3. It is only available on OS X/iPad

A. It is only available on OS X/iPad

Summary

In this chapter, we attempted to give a few additional pointers to you with regards to additional tools and technologies that could be useful complements to the core Neo4j graph database management system.

We covered additional tools around data integration, business intelligence tools, and modeling tools.

We hope this was a useful chapter and you are now ready to head into the final part of our book, that is, some useful appendices.

A
Where to Find More Information Related to Neo4j

Developing applications based on a radically new database architecture such as the Neo4j graph data model requires many different things. For sure, you will hit issues here and there, and at that point in time, you want to be able to find the right information quickly and efficiently. In this appendix, we will provide you with a short overview of potential information sources that could help you in this quest and give you a few pointers to useful information sources, quickly.

Online tools

The primary source of information for Neo4j is, of course, the online body of reference. Some of the most important parts of the Internet that could be of interest for you when getting started with Neo4j will be discussed next.

Google group

The Google forum at `https:// groups.google.com/group/neo4j` is a great place to ask questions, discuss experiences, and connect with other users of Neo4j. Because it leverages the Google search capabilities, it tends to be a great place for people to start looking for real-world experiences and advice.

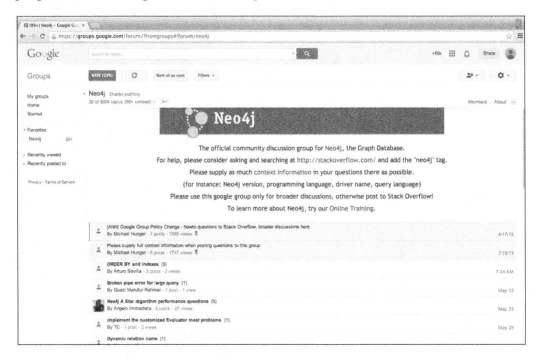

Stack Overflow

If or when you are looking for specific technical help or assistance, please consider asking a question on Stack Overflow. This is where you can get technical questions answered, either by the Community Management staff of Neo Technology or other volunteering contributors in the Neo4j community. Every question should have a neo4j tag, and then all of these questions and answers can be easily accessed by navigating to http://stackoverflow.com/questions/tagged/neo4j.

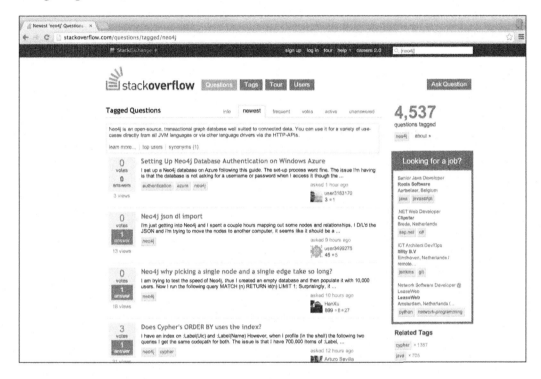

The Neo4j community website

For quite some time, the website of the Neo4j community, www.neo4j.org, has been a great resource with easily accessible information about the product, development practices, learning resources, and many other pieces of information. At the time of writing this, the website was about to be significantly redesigned.

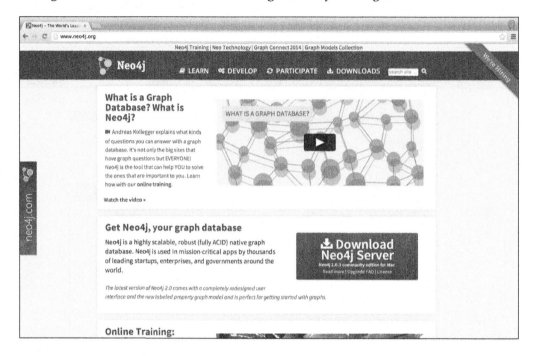

The new Neo4j website

At the time of writing of this chapter, Neo Technology was in the process of recreating a new website at www.neo4j.com, which would restructure and make information more accessible for a variety of audiences and give it a more pleasing look and feel. This process would include and merge both community and commercial resources, for both technical and more business-oriented contacts that want to inform themselves on Neo4j.

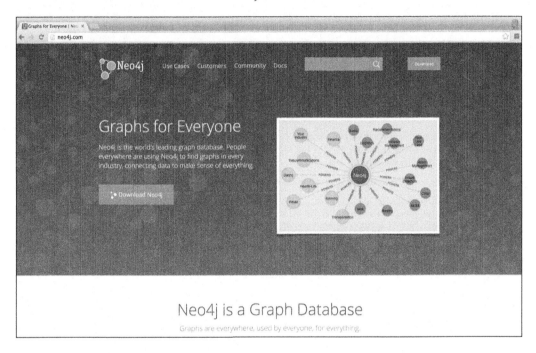

The Neo4j Blog

Many of the Neo4j developers and community members are fervent sharers of information, and much of what they write ends up on the Neo4j Blog. You can access the blog on the newly added blogging section of Neo4j at `http://neo4j.com/blog/`.

GraphGists collection

Since summer of 2013, Neo4j community members have started to share and publish some of their graph database models and use cases using a **GraphGist**. GraphGists use plain text files (formatted in AsciiDoc) available from any public URL (for example, GitHub gists) to create interactive, dynamically rendered graph examples and queries that are evaluated by a Neo4j infrastructure in the background. It allows great documentation and explanation of Neo4j models in an easily understandable way. Visit `http://gist.neo4j.org/` for many well-written examples of graph database use cases—there are a lot of them available on the website.

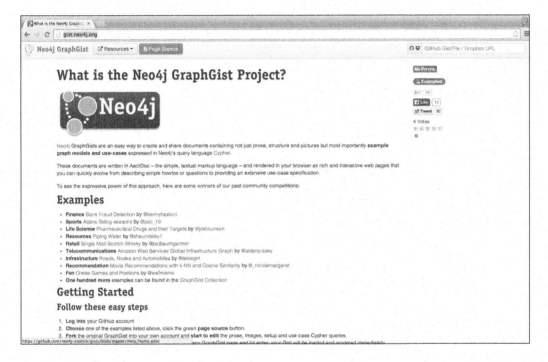

The Cypher reference card

Like many query languages, many users of it want and need to switch back to some kind of a reference for creating, maintaining, and/or troubleshooting specific kinds of queries. Cypher, the Neo4j declarative query language, therefore provides a handy reference page / card that many people turn to for occasional references. Visit `http://docs.neo4j.org/` for the most recent version (at the time of writing this, `http://docs.neo4j.org/refcard/2.1.2/` is the current one). You can always change the last digits to correspond to the presently generally available version of Neo4j.

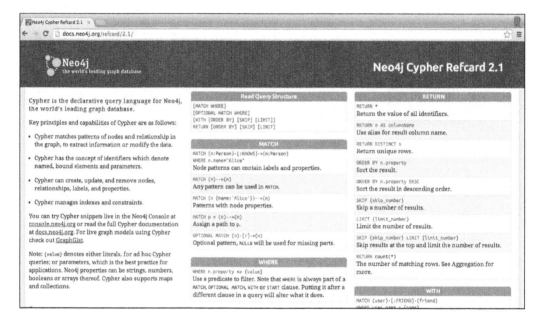

We will be including more information on Cypher in *Appendix B, Getting Started with Cypher.*

Other books

There are a number of interesting books on the market today that could provide good follow-up reading, now that you have almost finished *Learning Neo4j*. A few books to highlight are as follows:

- Another good book that specifically covers the Cypher query language is *Learning Cypher* by Packt Publishing (http://www.packtpub.com/learning-cypher/book).

- The O'Reilly book by Jim Webber, Ian Robinson, and Emil Eifrem. This book has been free to download at www.graphdatabases.com for a while, and still provides a good bit of detailed technical information.

- A book by OpenCredo's CEO Jonas Parter, published by Manning, *Neo4j in Action* (http://www.manning.com/partner/).

- A book by Michael Hunger and David Montag, published at InfoQ, *Good Relationships* (http://neo4j.com/books/good-relationships/).

No doubt there are other useful publications, but this should give you a good starting point.

Events

The Neo4j ecosystem, with Neo Technology as its more prominent supporter, organizes and participates in a very large number of events. You can find an overview of these events at http://neo4j.com/events, but there are a couple of event types that deserve a bit of additional attention and a separate mention.

Meetup

Most of the Neo4j community events are organized and administered through the Meetup website. You can find most groups quite easily at http://neo4j.meetup.com/ or by searching for it on the main website (www.meetup.com). Many of the meetups also have a standardized URL that should be something like www.meetup.com/graphdb-<your_city_name>.

GraphConnect

Since 2012, Neo Technology has been organizing an industry-wide conference called GraphConnect. In 2014, the conference will be hosted in San Francisco, and the current plan is to have a European conference in London early 2015. For the past few editions, it has attracted hundreds of graph databases users and enthusiasts (www.graphconnect.com).

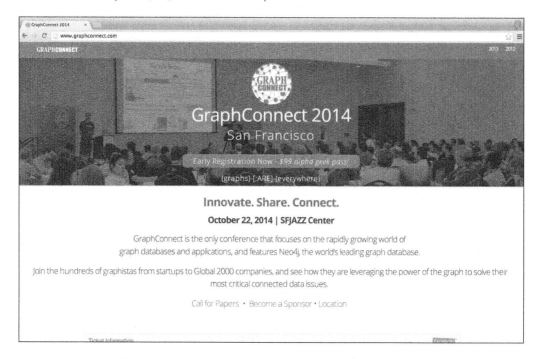

Conferences

Neo Technology attends a lot of interesting conferences around the world. You can find the most recent list of events at http://neo4j.com/events/#/events?area=Wo rld&type=Conference for more information.

Training

As more and more people start to deploy the Neo4j graph Database Management System, the need for building and managing the relevant competencies within the adopting enterprises will rise. Neo Technology has therefore started to provide different kinds of training that offer affordable and thorough possibilities for the users. You will find two types of training:

- **Classroom training**: These are available in many cities around the world. You can find an overview at `http://neo4j.com/events/#/events?area=World&type=Training`.

- **Online training**: Neo Technology started to offer online course material, for free, since early 2014. Given the success of the first training, it is very likely that additional courses will follow throughout the year. Visit `http://www.neo4j.org/learn/online_course` for the entry-level course as a starting point.

Neo Technology

As Neo Technology is the commercial backers of the Neo4j graph Database Management System, you can often also get very useful input from the friendly folds at Neo Technology. They try to help you whenever possible, and you can often benefit most if you reach out to them earlier rather than later. You can use the contact form at `http://www.neotechnology.com/contact-us-form/` to do so, or send an e-mail to `info@neotechnology.com`.

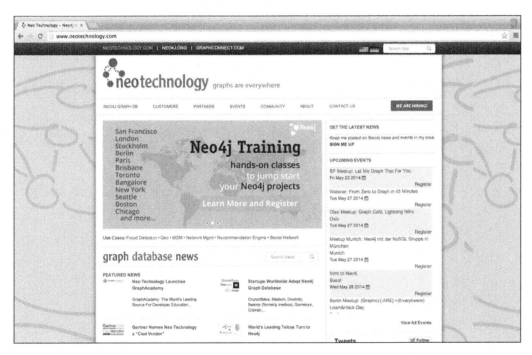

Neo Technology is also building a partner network with integrators and consultancy organizations that have expertise and an active interest in the Neo4j graph Database Management System. You can find the list of partners at `http://www.neotechnology.com/partners/`, but given the fact that this list is rapidly changing and growing at the time of writing this, you would probably get a more accurate view of the current landscape by contacting Neo Technology themselves and letting them help you find the appropriate partner.

B

Getting Started with Cypher

Database systems need query languages in order for humans and software applications to interact with them in an efficient way. There are a number of graph query languages out there already (Gremlin and SparQL, to name just two), and some of these have certainly inspired the creation of Cypher, but Cypher is quite different than anything else you may have come across before. No book on Neo4j would be complete without at least spending some time on it—in spite of the fact that there are entire books, presentations, and courses available for you to review.

The key attributes of Cypher

In making Cypher, Neo Technology and Andres Taylor (@andres_taylor) set out to create a new query language, specifically for dealing with graph data structures like the ones we store in Neo4j. There were a couple of reasons for doing this, more specifically four attributes that are not available together in any other query language out there.

Let's quickly examine these attributes, as they are quite important to understanding the way Cypher works in Neo4j:

- **Declarative**: Cypher is a declarative query language, which is very different from the imperative alternatives out there. You *declare* the pattern that you are looking for. You effectively tell Cypher what you want, not how to get it. This is crucial, as imperative approaches always suppose that you—as you interact with the database—have the following qualities:
    - A programmer who knows how to tell the database what to do—probably with some procedural logic that would need to be formalized in a program

° Someone that intimately knows the structure, size, and semantics of the dataset being queried in order for the imperative path to the result set to be optimally formed

Both assumptions seem to be quite far-fetched and for this reason, many database systems have settled on declarative approaches to querying their data. **Structured Query Language (SQL)** is of course the most well known example.

- **Expressive**: Many people have highlighted that the Cypher syntax is a little bit like ASCII art, and it probably is. With its rounded and square brackets, and the arrows connecting the parts of the pattern, it is very easy to understand how the query language expresses what you are looking for. The reason behind optimizing the syntax for reading is simple and clear: most code gets read far more often than that it gets written. Expressiveness, therefore, is a very interesting attribute for teams working together on a system that relies on the Neo4j graph Database Management System.

- **Pattern Matching**: Cypher is a pattern matching query language. This is probably one of the more "graphy" aspects of the language, as it allows people to sketch and draw complex relationships between different entities in the data set quite easily. Humans are actually very good at working with patterns; it tends to be very easy for our brain to work with them. Many people therefore experience cypher as a very easy query language to get started with.

- **Idempotent**: When Neo Technology started working on Cypher, the lead architect of the query language, Andres Taylor, set out to do so using Scala, a functional programming language on the Java Virtual Machine. One of the key traits of functional programing environments is that they are supposed to be idempotent. In layman's terms, this means that when you operate a function (or in our case, execute a query) in your algorithm, changes in the data should only happen on the first execution of the function. Multiple executions of the same function over the same data should have no effect. This has some great advantages in functional programs, but also in the Neo4j database, as state change will be expressed idempotently.

Knowing this, we can now explore some of the key operative words in Cypher, and familiarize you with some of these concepts in the real world.

Key operative words in Cypher

Like every database query language, there are a few operative words that have an important meaning in the composition of every query. It's useful for you to know these since you will be using them to compose your specific queries on your specific datasets.

Keyword	Function	Example
MATCH	This describes a pattern that the database should match. This is probably the most important piece of the query as it is a structural component that always starts your queries.	`MATCH (me:Person)-[:KNOWS]->(friend)`
WHERE	This filters results that are found in the match for specific criteria.	`WHERE me.name = "My Name" AND me.age > 18`
RETURN	This returns results. You can either return paths, nodes, relationships, or their properties — or an aggregate of the mentioned parameters. This is another structural component, as all read queries and most write queries will return some data.	`RETURN me.name, collect(friend), count(*) as friends`
WITH	This passes results from one query part to the next. Much like RETURN, but instead of including data in the result set, it will be passed to the following part of the query. It transforms and aggregates results and also separates READ and UPDATE statements.	
ORDER BY SKIP LIMIT:	This sorts and paginates the results.	`ORDER BY friends DESC SKIP 10 LIMIT 10`
CREATE	This creates nodes and relationships with their properties.	`CREATE (p:Person), (p)-[:KNOWS {since: 2010}]-> (me:Person {name:"My Name"})`
CREATE UNIQUE	This fixes graph structures by only creating structures if they do not yet exist.	

Keyword	Function	Example
MERGE	This matches or creates semantics by using indexes and locks. You can specify different operations in case of a MATCH (part of the pattern already existed) or on CREATE (pattern did not exist yet).	MERGE (me:Person {name:"My Name"}) ON MATCH me SET me.accessed = timestamp() ON CREATE me SET me.age = 42
SET, REMOVE	This updates properties and labels on nodes and/or relationships.	SET me.age = 42 SET me:Employee REMOVE me.first_name REMOVE me:Contractor
DELETE	It deletes nodes and relationships.	MATCH (me) OPTIONAL MATCH (me)-[r]-() DELETE me, r

With these simple keywords, you should be able to start forming your first Cypher queries. After all, it's a bit like ASCII art, a structure similar to the one shown in the following diagram:

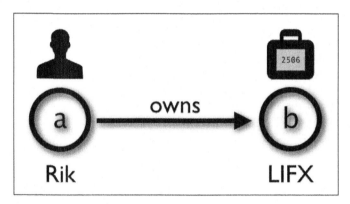

This is very easily described in Cypher as:

```
(a:Person {name:"Rik")-[:OWNS]->(b:Device {brand:"LIFX"})
```

All we need to do to make this a proper Cypher statement is to wrap it in MATCH and RETURN statements:

```
Match
(a:Person {name:"Rik")-[r:OWNS]->(b:Device {brand:"LIFX"})
return a,r,b;
```

This is just a simple example of how you would start using Cypher. More complex examples can of course be found elsewhere in this book. You can also find the complete Cypher Ref Card (online version at http://docs.neo4j.org/refcard/2.1/) included in the final pages of this book.

The Cypher refcard

Cypher is the declarative query language for Neo4j, the world's leading graph database.

The key principles and capabilities of Cypher are as follows:

- Cypher matches patterns of nodes and relationship in the graph, to extract information or modify the data
- Cypher has the concept of identifiers, which denote named, bound elements and parameters
- Cypher can create, update, and remove nodes, relationships, labels, and properties
- Cypher manages indexes and constraints

You can try Cypher snippets live in the Neo4j Console at console.neo4j.org or read the full Cypher documentation at docs.neo4j.org. For live graph models using Cypher, check out the graph gists at gist.neo4j.org as well.

> {value} denotes either literals (for ad hoc Cypher queries) or parameters, which is the best practice for applications. Neo4j properties can be strings, numbers, Booleans, or arrays. Cypher also supports maps and collections.

For your convenience, we included the online version of the Cypher refcard (http://docs.neo4j.org/refcard/2.1.1/) in unaltered form in this book. This refcard is published online under the Creative Commons Attribution-ShareAlike 3.0 Unported (CC BY-SA 3.0) license, details of which can be found at http://creativecommons.org/licenses/by-sa/3.0/.

Syntax

The following table shows the syntax of various operators:

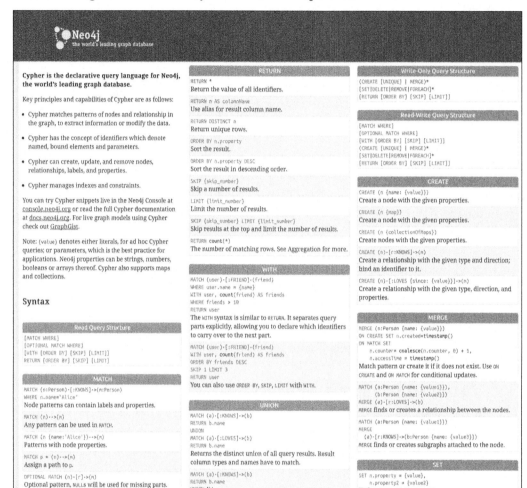

Cypher is the declarative query language for Neo4j, the world's leading graph database.

Key principles and capabilities of Cypher are as follows:

- Cypher matches patterns of nodes and relationship in the graph, to extract information or modify the data.
- Cypher has the concept of identifiers which denote named, bound elements and parameters.
- Cypher can create, update, and remove nodes, relationships, labels, and properties.
- Cypher manages indexes and constraints.

You can try Cypher snippets live in the Neo4j Console at console.neo4j.org or read the full Cypher documentation at docs.neo4j.org. For live graph models using Cypher check out GraphGist.

Note: (value) denotes either literals, for ad hoc Cypher queries; or parameters, which is the best practice for applications. Neo4j properties can be strings, numbers, booleans or arrays thereof. Cypher also supports maps and collections.

Syntax

Read Query Structure

```
[MATCH WHERE]
[OPTIONAL MATCH WHERE]
[WITH [ORDER BY] [SKIP] [LIMIT]]
RETURN [ORDER BY] [SKIP] [LIMIT]
```

MATCH

```
MATCH (n:Person)-[:KNOWS]->(m:Person)
WHERE n.name="Alice"
```
Node patterns can contain labels and properties.

```
MATCH (n)-->(m)
```
Any pattern can be used in MATCH.

```
MATCH (n {name:'Alice'})-->(m)
```
Patterns with node properties.

```
MATCH p = (n)-->(m)
```
Assign a path to p.

```
OPTIONAL MATCH (n)-[r]->(m)
```
Optional pattern, NULLS will be used for missing parts.

RETURN

```
RETURN *
```
Return the value of all identifiers.

```
RETURN n AS columnName
```
Use alias for result column name.

```
RETURN DISTINCT n
```
Return unique rows.

```
ORDER BY n.property
```
Sort the result.

```
ORDER BY n.property DESC
```
Sort the result in descending order.

```
SKIP {skip_number}
```
Skip a number of results.

```
LIMIT {limit_number}
```
Limit the number of results.

```
SKIP {skip_number} LIMIT {limit_number}
```
Skip results at the top and limit the number of results.

```
RETURN count(*)
```
The number of matching rows. See Aggregation for more.

WITH

```
MATCH (user)-[:FRIEND]-(friend)
WHERE user.name = {name}
WITH user, count(friend) AS friends
WHERE friends > 10
RETURN user
```
The WITH syntax is similar to RETURN. It separates query parts explicitly, allowing you to declare which identifiers to carry over to the next part.

```
MATCH (user)-[:FRIEND]-(friend)
WITH user, count(friend) AS friends
ORDER BY friends DESC
SKIP 1 LIMIT 3
RETURN user
```
You can also use ORDER BY, SKIP, LIMIT with WITH.

UNION

```
MATCH (a)-[:KNOWS]->(b)
RETURN b.name
UNION
MATCH (a)-[:LOVES]->(b)
RETURN b.name
```
Returns the distinct union of all query results. Result column types and names have to match.

```
MATCH (a)-[:KNOWS]->(b)
RETURN b.name
UNION ALL
```

Write-Only Query Structure

```
(CREATE [UNIQUE] | MERGE)*
[SET|DELETE|REMOVE|FOREACH]*
[RETURN [ORDER BY] [SKIP] [LIMIT]]
```

Read-Write Query Structure

```
[MATCH WHERE]
[OPTIONAL MATCH WHERE]
[WITH [ORDER BY] [SKIP] [LIMIT]]
(CREATE [UNIQUE] | MERGE)*
[SET|DELETE|REMOVE|FOREACH]*
[RETURN [ORDER BY] [SKIP] [LIMIT]]
```

CREATE

```
CREATE (n {name: {value}})
```
Create a node with the given properties.

```
CREATE (n {map})
```
Create a node with the given properties.

```
CREATE (n {collectionOfMaps})
```
Create nodes with the given properties.

```
CREATE (n)-[:KNOWS]->(m)
```
Create a relationship with the given type and direction; bind an identifier to it.

```
CREATE (n)-[:LOVES {since: {value}}]->(n)
```
Create a relationship with the given type, direction, and properties.

MERGE

```
MERGE (n:Person {name: {value}})
ON CREATE SET n.created=timestamp()
ON MATCH SET
    n.counter= coalesce(n.counter, 0) + 1,
    n.accessTime = timestamp()
```
Match pattern or create it if it does not exist. Use ON CREATE and ON MATCH for conditional updates.

```
MATCH (a:Person {name: {value1}}),
      (b:Person {name: {value2}})
MERGE (a)-[r:LOVES]->(b)
```
MERGE finds or creates a relationship between the nodes.

```
MATCH (a:Person {name: {value1}})
MERGE
    (a)-[r:KNOWS]->(b:Person {name: {value3}})
```
MERGE finds or creates subgraphs attached to the node.

SET

```
SET n.property = {value},
    n.property2 = {value2}
```
Update or create a property.

WHERE

```
WHERE n.property <> {value}
```
Use a predicate to filter. Note that WHERE is always part of a MATCH, OPTIONAL MATCH, WITH or START clause. Putting it after a different clause in a query will alter what it does.

Operators

Mathematical	+, -, *, /, %, ^
Comparison	=, <>, <, >, <=, >=
Boolean	AND, OR, XOR, NOT
String	+
Collection	+, IN, [x], [x .. y]
Regular Expression	=~

NULL

- NULL is used to represent missing/undefined values.
- NULL is not equal to NULL. Not knowing two values does not imply that they are the same value. So the expression NULL = NULL yields NULL and not TRUE. To check if an expressoin is NULL, use IS NULL.
- Arithmetic expressions, comparisons and function calls (except coalesce) will return NULL if any argument is NULL.
- Missing elements like a property that doesn't exist or accessing elements that don't exist in a collection yields NULL.
- In OPTIONAL MATCH clauses, NULLs will be used for missing parts of the pattern.

CASE

```
CASE n.eyes
  WHEN 'blue' THEN 1
  WHEN 'brown' THEN 2
  ELSE 3
END
```
Return THEN value from the matching WHEN value. The ELSE value is optional, and substituted for NULL if missing.

```
CASE
  WHEN n.eyes = 'blue' THEN 1
  WHEN n.age < 40 THEN 2
  ELSE 3
END
```
Return THEN value from the first WHEN predicate evaluating to TRUE. Predicates are evaluated in order.

```
MATCH (a)-[:LOVES]->(b)
RETURN b.name
```
Returns the union of all query results, including duplicated rows.

Collections

```
['a','b','c'] AS coll
```
Literal collections are declared in square brackets.

```
length({coll}) AS len, {coll}[0] AS value
```
Collections can be passed in as parameters.

```
range({first_num},{last_num},{step}) AS coll
```
Range creates a collection of numbers (step is optional). other functions returning collections are: labels, nodes, relationships, rels, filter, extract.

```
MATCH (a)-[r:KNOWS*]->()
RETURN r AS rels
```
Relationship identifiers of a variable length path contain a collection of relationships.

```
RETURN matchedNode.coll[0] AS value,
       length(matchedNode.coll) AS len
```
Properties can be arrays/collections of strings, numbers or booleans.

```
coll[{idx}] AS value,
coll[{start_idx}]..{end_idx}] AS slice
```
Collection elements can be accessed with idx subscripts in square brackets. Invalid indexes return NULL. Slices can be retrieved with intervals from start_idx to end_idx each of which can be omitted or negative. Out of range elements are ignored.

```
UNWIND {names} AS name
MATCH (n {name:name})
RETURN avg(n.age)
```
With UNWIND, you can transform any collection back into individual rows. The example matches all names from a list of names.

Performance

- Use parameters instead of literals when possible. This allows Cypher to re-use your queries instead of having to parse and build new execution plans.
- Always set an upper limit for your variable length patterns. It's easy to have a query go wild and touch all nodes in a graph by mistake.
- Return only the data you need. Avoid returning whole nodes and relationships — instead, pick the data you need and return only that.

```
SET n = {map}
```
Set all properties. This will remove any existing properties.

```
SET n += {map}
```
Add and update properties, while keeping existing ones.

```
SET n:Person
```
Adds a label Person to a node.

DELETE

```
DELETE n, r
```
Delete a node and a relationship.

REMOVE

```
REMOVE n:Person
```
Remove a label from n.

```
REMOVE n.property
```
Remove a property.

INDEX

```
CREATE INDEX ON :Person(name)
```
Create an index on the label Person and property name.

```
MATCH (n:Person) WHERE n.name = {value}
```
An index can be automatically used for the equality comparison. Note that for example lower(n.name) = {value} will not use an index.

```
MATCH (n:Person) WHERE n.name IN [{value}]
```
An index can be automatically used for the IN collection checks.

```
MATCH (n:Person)
USING INDEX n:Person(name)
WHERE n.name = {value}
```
Index usage can be enforced, when Cypher uses a suboptimal index or more than one index should be used.

```
DROP INDEX ON :Person(name)
```
Drop the index on the label Person and property name.

CONSTRAINT

```
CREATE CONSTRAINT ON (p:Person)
       ASSERT p.name IS UNIQUE
```
Create a unique constraint on the label Person and property name. If any other node with that label is updated or created with a name that already exists, the write operation will fail. This constraint will create an accompanying index.

```
DROP CONSTRAINT ON (p:Person)
       ASSERT p.name IS UNIQUE
```
Drop the unique constraint and index on the label Person and property name.

Neo4j Cypher Refcard 2.1.2

Patterns

`(n)-->(n)`
A relationship from n to n exists.

`(n:Person)`
Matches nodes with the label Person.

`(n:Person:Swedish)`
Matches nodes which have both Person and Swedish labels.

`(n:Person {name: {value}})`
Matches nodes with the declared properties.

`(n:Person)-->(m)`
Node n labeled Person has a relationship to m.

`(n)--(m)`
A relationship in any direction between n and m.

`(n)<-[:KNOWS]-(n)`
A relationship from n to n of type KNOWS exists.

`(n)-[:KNOWS|LOVES]->(m)`
A relationship from n to m of type KNOWS or LOVES exists.

`(n)-[r]->(m)`
Bind an identifier to the relationship.

`(n)-[*1..5]->(m)`
Variable length paths.

`(n)-[*]->(m)`
Any depth. See the performance tips.

`(n)-[:KNOWS]->(m {property: {value}})`
Match or set properties in MATCH, CREATE, CREATE UNIQUE or MERGE clauses.

`shortestPath((n1:Person)-[*..6]-(n2:Person))`
Find a single shortest path.

`allShortestPaths((n1:Person)-->(n2:Person))`
Find all shortest paths.

Labels

`CREATE (n:Person {name:{value}})`
Create a node with label and property.

`MERGE (n:Person {name:{value}})`
Matches or creates unique node(s) with label and property.

`SET n:Spouse:Parent:Employee`
Add label(s) to a node.

`MATCH (n:Person)`

Maps

`{name:'Alice', age:38,`
`  address:{city:'London', residential:true}}`
Literal maps are declared in curly braces much like property maps. Nested maps and collections are supported.

`MERGE (p:Person {name: {map}.name})`
`ON CREATE SET p={map}`
Maps can be passed in as parameters and used as map or by accessing keys.

`MATCH (matchedNode:Person)`
`RETURN matchedNode`
Nodes and relationships are returned as maps of their data.

`map.name, map.age, map.children[0]`
Map entries can be accessed by their keys. Invalid keys result in an error.

Relationship Functions

`type(a_relationship)`
String representation of the relationship type.

`startNode(a_relationship)`
Start node of the relationship.

`endNode(a_relationship)`
End node of the relationship.

`id(a_relationship)`
The internal id of the relationship.

Collection Predicates

`all(x IN coll WHERE has(x.property))`
Returns true if the predicate is TRUE for all elements of the collection.

`any(x IN coll WHERE has(x.property))`
Returns true if the predicate is TRUE for at least one element of the collection.

`none(x IN coll WHERE has(x.property))`
Returns TRUE if the predicate is FALSE for all elements of the collection.

`single(x IN coll WHERE has(x.property))`
Returns TRUE if the predicate is TRUE for exactly one element in the collection.

Path Functions

`length(path)`
The length of the path.

`nodes(path)`
The nodes in the path as a collection.

`relationships(path)`
The relationships in the path as a collection.

`MATCH path=(n)-->(m)`
`RETURN extract(x IN nodes(path) | x.prop)`
Assign a path and process its nodes.

`MATCH path = (begin) -[*]-> (end)`
`FOREACH`
`  (n IN rels(path) | SET n.marked = TRUE)`
Execute a mutating operation for each relationship of a path.

Collection Functions

`length({coll})`
Length of the collection.

`head({coll}), last({coll}), tail({coll})`
head returns the first, last the last element of the collection. tail the remainder of the collection. All return null for an empty collection.

`[x IN coll WHERE x.prop <> {value} | x.prop]`
Combination of filter and extract in a concise notation.

`extract(x IN coll | x.prop)`
A collection of the value of the expression for each element in the orignal collection.

`filter(x IN coll WHERE x.prop <> {value})`
A filtered collection of the elements where the predicate is TRUE.

`reduce(s = "", x IN coll | s + x.prop)`
Evaluate expression for each element in the collection, accumulate the results.

`FOREACH (value IN coll |`
`  CREATE (:Person {name:value}))`
Execute a mutating operation for each element in a collection.

Aggregation

`count(*)`
The number of matching rows.

Matches nodes labeled as Person.

```
MATCH (n:Person)
WHERE n.name = {value}
```
Matches nodes labeled Person with the given name.

```
WHERE (n:Person)
```
Checks existence of label on node.

```
labels(n)
```
Labels of the node.

```
REMOVE n:Person
```
Remove label from node.

Predicates

```
n.property <> {value}
```
Use comparison operators.

```
has(n.property)
```
Use functions.

```
n.number >= 1 AND n.number <= 10
```
Use boolean operators to combine predicates.

```
n:Person
```
Check for node labels.

```
identifier IS NULL
```
Check if something is NULL.

```
NOT has(n.property) OR n.property = {value}
```
Either property does not exist or predicate is TRUE.

```
n.property = {value}
```
Non-existing property returns NULL, which is not equal to anything.

```
n.property =~ "Tob.*"
```
Regular expression.

```
(n)-[:KNOWS]->(m)
```
Make sure the pattern has at least one match.

```
NOT (n)-[:KNOWS]->(m)
```
Exclude matches to (n)-[:KNOWS]->(m) from the result.

```
n.property IN [{value1}, {value2}]
```
Check if an element exists in a collection.

Functions

```
coalesce(n.property, {defaultValue})
```
The first non-NULL expression.

```
timestamp()
```
Milliseconds since midnight, January 1, 1970 UTC.

```
id(node_or_relationship)
```
The internal id of the relationship or node.

```
toInt({expr})
```
Converts the given input in an integer if possible; otherwise it returns NULL.

```
toFloat({expr})
```
Converts the given input in a floating point number if possible; otherwise it returns NULL.

Mathematical Functions

```
abs({expr})
```
The absolute value.

```
rand()
```
A random value. Returns a new value for each call. Also useful for selecting subset or random ordering.

```
round({expr})
```
Round to the nearest integer, ceil and floor find the next integer up or down.

```
sqrt({expr})
```
The square root.

```
sign({expr})
```
0 if zero, -1 if negative, 1 if positive.

```
sin({expr})
```
Trigonometric functions, also cos, tan, cot, asin, acos, atan, atan2, haversin.

```
degrees({expr}), radians({expr}), pi()
```
Converts radians into degrees, use radians for the reverse. pi for π.

```
log10({expr}), log({expr}), exp({expr}), e()
```
Logarithm base 10, natural logarithm, e to the power of the parameter. Value of e.

String Functions

```
str({expression})
```
String representation of the expression.

```
replace({original}, {search}, {replacement})
```
Replace all occurrences of search with replacement. All arguments are be expressions.

```
substring({original}, {begin}, {sub_length})
```
Get part of a string. The sub_length argument is optional.

```
left({original}, {sub_length}),
    right({original}, {sub_length})
```
The first part of a string. The last part of the string.

```
trim({original}), ltrim({original}),
    rtrim({original})
```
Trim all whitespace, or on left or right side.

```
upper({original}), lower({original})
```
UPPERCASE and lowercase.

```
split({original}, {delimiter})
```
Split a string into a collection of strings.

START

```
START n=node(*)
```
Start from all nodes.

```
START n=node({ids})
```
Start from one or more nodes specified by id.

```
START n=node({id1}), n=node({id2})
```
Multiple starting points.

```
START n=node:nodeIndexName(key={value})
```
Query the index with an exact query. Use node_auto_index for the automatic index.

```
count(identifier)
```
The number of non-NULL values.

```
count(DISTINCT identifier)
```
All aggregation functions also take the DISTINCT modifier, which removes duplicates from the values.

```
collect(n.property)
```
Collection from the values, ignores NULL.

```
sum(n.property)
```
Sum numerical values. Similar functions are avg, min, max.

```
percentileDisc(n.property, {percentile})
```
Discrete percentile. Continuous percentile is percentileCont. The percentile argument is from 0.0 to 1.0.

```
stdev(n.property)
```
Standard deviation for a sample of a population. For an entire population use stdevp.

Upgrading

With Neo4j 2.0 several Cypher features in version 1.9 have been deprecated or removed.

- START is optional.
- MERGE will take CREATE UNIQUE's role for the unique creation of patterns. Note that they are not the same, though.
- Optional relationships are handled by OPTIONAL MATCH, not question marks.
- Non-existing properties return NULL, n.prop? and n.prop! have been removed.
- The separator for collection functions changed from : to |.
- Paths are no longer collections, use nodes(path) or rels(path).
- Parentheses around nodes in patterns are no longer optional.
- CREATE a={property:'value'} has been removed.
- Use REMOVE to remove properties.
- Parameters for index-keys and nodes in patterns are no longer allowed.
- To still use the older syntax, prepend your Cypher statement with CYPHER 1.9.

CREATE UNIQUE

```
CREATE UNIQUE
    (n)-[:KNOWS]->(m {property: {value}})
```
Match pattern or create it if it does not exist. The pattern can not include any optional parts.

Index

Thank you for buying
Learning Neo4j

About Packt Publishing

Packt, pronounced 'packed', published its first book "*Mastering phpMyAdmin for Effective MySQL Management*" in April 2004 and subsequently continued to specialize in publishing highly focused books on specific technologies and solutions.

Our books and publications share the experiences of your fellow IT professionals in adapting and customizing today's systems, applications, and frameworks. Our solution based books give you the knowledge and power to customize the software and technologies you're using to get the job done. Packt books are more specific and less general than the IT books you have seen in the past. Our unique business model allows us to bring you more focused information, giving you more of what you need to know, and less of what you don't.

Packt is a modern, yet unique publishing company, which focuses on producing quality, cutting-edge books for communities of developers, administrators, and newbies alike. For more information, please visit our website: www.packtpub.com.

About Packt Open Source

In 2010, Packt launched two new brands, Packt Open Source and Packt Enterprise, in order to continue its focus on specialization. This book is part of the Packt Open Source brand, home to books published on software built around Open Source licenses, and offering information to anybody from advanced developers to budding web designers. The Open Source brand also runs Packt's Open Source Royalty Scheme, by which Packt gives a royalty to each Open Source project about whose software a book is sold.

Writing for Packt

We welcome all inquiries from people who are interested in authoring. Book proposals should be sent to author@packtpub.com. If your book idea is still at an early stage and you would like to discuss it first before writing a formal book proposal, contact us; one of our commissioning editors will get in touch with you.

We're not just looking for published authors; if you have strong technical skills but no writing experience, our experienced editors can help you develop a writing career, or simply get some additional reward for your expertise.

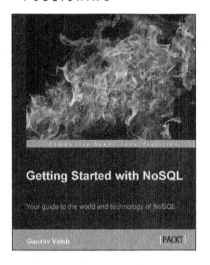

Getting Started with NoSQL

Your guide to the world and technology of NoSQL

Gaurav Vaish   PACKT

Getting Started with NoSQL

ISBN: 978-1-84969-498-8   Paperback: 142 pages

Your guide to the world and technology of NoSQL

1. First hand, detailed information about NoSQL technology.

2. Learn the differences between NoSQL and RDBMS and where each is useful.

3. Understand the various data models for NoSQL.

4. Compare and contrast some of the popular NoSQL databases on the market.

5. Think outside the box; learn to design, construct, and implement using NoSQL.

Learn by doing: less theory, more results

CouchDB and PHP
Web Development

Get your PHP application from conception to deployment by leveraging CouchDB's robust features

Beginner's Guide

Tim Juravich   [   ] open source

CouchDB and PHP Web Development Beginner's Guide

ISBN: 978-1-84951-358-6   Paperback: 304 pages

Get your PHP application from conception to deployment by leveraging CouchDB's robust features

1. Build and deploy a flexible Social Networking application using PHP and leveraging key features of CouchDB to do the heavy lifting.

2. Explore the features and functionality of CouchDB, by taking a deep look into Documents, Views, Replication, and much more.

3. Conceptualize a lightweight PHP framework from scratch and write code that can easily port to other frameworks.

Please check **www.PacktPub.com** for information on our titles

Getting Started with MariaDB

Getting Started with
MariaDB

ISBN: 978-1-78216-809-6   Paperback: 100 pages

Learn how to use MariaDB to store your data easily
and hassle-free

1. A step-by-step guide to installing and
    configuring MariaDB.

2. Includes real-world examples that help
    you learn how to store and maintain data
    on MariaDB.

3. Written by someone who has been involved
    with the project since its inception.

Pentaho Analytics for MongoDB

ISBN: 978-1-78216-835-5   Paperback: 146 pages

Combine Pentaho Analytics and MongoDB to create
powerful analysis and reporting solutions

1. This is a step-by-step guide that will have
    you quickly creating eye-catching data
    visualizations.

2. Includes a sample MongoDB database of web
    clickstream events for learning how to model
    and query MongoDB data.

3. Full of tips, images, and exercises that cover
    the Pentaho development life cycle.

Please check **www.PacktPub.com** for information on our titles

CPSIA information can be obtained at www.ICGtesting.com
Printed in the USA
BVOW08s2008080914

365974BV00003B/3/P